PHONES DOWN BIBLE Activity Fun

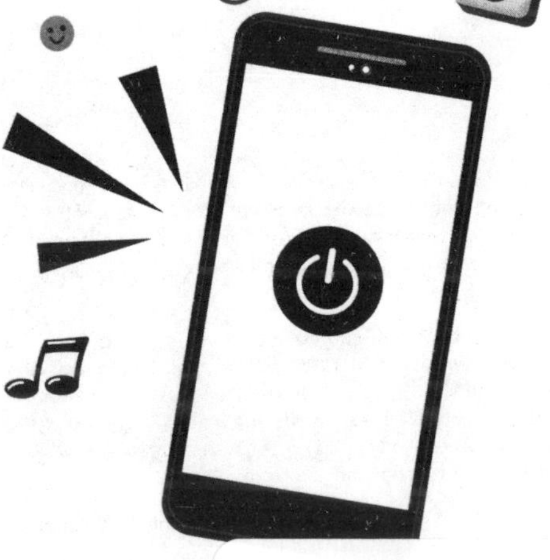

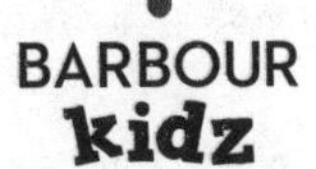

A Division of Barbour Publishing

Puzzles created by Jennifer Hahn

ISBN 979-8-89151-144-6

Published by Barbour Publishing, Inc., 1810 Barbour Drive, Uhrichsville, Ohio 44683, www.barbourbooks.com

Our mission is to inspire the world with the life-changing message of the Bible.

Printed in the United States of America.

002614 0625 CM

PHONES DOWN
Bible Activity Fun!

Perfect for kids ages 6 to 10, this book is jam-packed with Bible-based pencil-and-paper games to challenge and amuse, to entertain and educate.

Here are more than 100 crosswords, word searches, secret codes, fill-in-the-blanks, and picture fun pages, covering the entire Bible from Genesis to Revelation.

Inside, you'll find the following types of puzzles:

- ***Crosswords***: Fill in the puzzle grid by answering the "across" and "down" clues. If you need help, verse references are provided.
- ***Word searches***: In the puzzle grid, find and circle the **bolded** search words in the scripture—the words might run forward, backward, up, down, or on the diagonal.
- ***Decoders***: For every two-digit number in the puzzle, find the correct letter in the decoder grid. The first number refers to the row (the numbers running down the left side of the grid). The second number indicates the column (the numbers running across the top of the grid). After you've determined all the letters and placed them in the puzzle, they'll spell out an important verse.
- ***Acrostics***: Read the definition in the left-hand column and write the word it describes in the right-hand column. Then place the coded letters from the right-hand column into the puzzle below to spell out a Bible verse.
- ***Picture fun***: Solve a maze, connect the dots, finish the picture. . .and color them all!

If you're looking for something fun to do, grab a pencil or pen and jump into *Phones Down Bible Activity Fun*!

NOTE:

This book quotes Bible verses from the King James Version, the New Life Version, and the Barbour Simplified KJV Bible. You can find the first two online at **BibleGateway.com**; the third is available at **simplifiedkjv.com**.

ACROSTIC

1. God's First Creation

GENESIS 1:1–27 NLV

God created everything from ___ (1:1)	24–12–1–7–5–9–3
The ___ were divided by an open space (1:6)	2–20–15–26–22–17
Plants and trees produce ___ (1:11)	10–19–23–4–27
___ are found in the air (1:20)	6–11–21–25–13
Another word for a man (1:27)	16–14–18–8

15–7–26–9 3–12–25 13–20–5–25, "18–8–15 1–7–26–22–8 6–23 18–11–3–7–1," 14–9–25 1–7–8–21–8 2–14–13 18–5–3–7–15.

WORD SEARCH

2. God Creates Humans

GENESIS 1:26–27 KJV

And **God** said, Let us **make** man in our **image**, after our **likeness**: and let them have **dominion** over the **fish** of the sea, and over the **fowl** of the air, and over the **cattle**, and over all the **earth**, and over every **creeping** thing that creepeth upon the earth. So God **created** man in his own image, in the image of God created he him; **male** and **female** created he them.

CROSSWORD

3. Creation Week

Genesis 1–2 SKJV

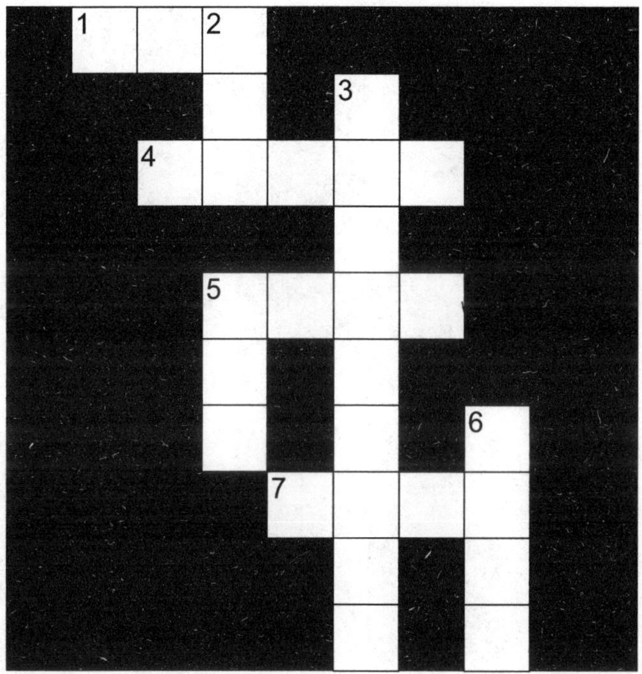

Across

1. On day ___, God created "Heaven"—or the sky (1:6–8)
4. On day ___, God rested (2:1–3)
5. What God did to create all things (1:3, 6, 9, and so on!)
7. On day ___, God created ocean animals and birds (1:20–23)

Down

2. On day ___, God created light (1:3–5)
3. When God created everything (1:1)
5. On day ___, God created land animals and humans (1:24–31)
6. All of God's creation was ___ good (1:31)

CROSSWORD

4. The Seventh Day of Creation

GENESIS 2:1–3 NLV

Across

3. They were completed on the seventh day (2:1)
6. What God did to the seventh day (2:3)
7. What God said the seventh day was (2:3)

Down

1. Another word for "finished" (2:3)
2. "And [God] _____ on the seventh day" (2:2)
4. It was completed on the seventh day (2:1)
5. What God ended on the seventh day (2:2)

COLORING PAGE

5. Adam, Eve, and the Serpent

WORD SEARCH

6. The First Sin

GENESIS 3:2–6 SKJV

And the woman said to the **serpent**, "We may eat of the fruit from the trees of the **garden**, but of the fruit of the tree that is in the **midst** of the garden, God has said, 'You shall not eat from it, neither shall you touch it, lest you die.'"

And the serpent said to the **woman**, "You shall not surely die, for God knows that in the day you eat from it, then your eyes shall be opened and you shall be as gods, **knowing good** and **evil**."

And when the woman saw that the tree was good for food, and that it was **pleasant** to the **eyes**, and a tree to be desired to make one **wise**, she took some of its **fruit** and ate, and gave also to her **husband** with her, and he ate.

WORD SEARCH

7. Trees of the Bible

Adam and Eve ate fruit from the Tree of Knowledge of Good and Evil. What are some other trees noted in the Bible?

Fig (Deuteronomy 8:8)
Olive (Deuteronomy 6:11)
Cedar (1 Kings 5:6)
Sycamore (1 Kings 10:27)
Acacia (Exodus 36:20)
Oak (Judges 6:11)
Willow (Ezekiel 17:5)
Palm (Psalm 92:12)
Broom (Psalm 120:4)
Almond (Jeremiah 1:11)
Chestnut (Ezekiel 31:8)
Juniper (1 Kings 19:4)

All names from the New Life Version.

ACROSTIC

8. Building the Ark

GENESIS 6:14–16, 22 SKJV

"Make an ark of ____ wood" (6:14) 12–23–5–36–26–15

"You shall make ____ in the ark" (6:14) 29–10–40–17–8

"Pitch it inside and ____ with pitch" (6:14) 32–3–43–21–16–33–44

The ark's height was to be thirty ____ (6:15) 19–4–22–37–42–14

The ark was to be ____hundred cubits long (6:15) 20–6–31–28–13

The ark's breadth was to be ____ cubits (6:15) 39–2–18–27–41

"You shall make a ____ to the ark" (6:16) 24–38–1–9–30–35

"The door of the ark you ____ set in its side" (6:16) 11–34–7–25–45

20–6–3–21 1–23–7–36 33–38–9, 7–19–19–10–15–33–38–1–12

20–32 7–45–25 20–34–7–43 12–32–9 19–30–17–17–7–1–33–44–9

36–38–17, 8–40 6–26 9–16–33.

CROSSWORD

9. Boarding the Ark

GENESIS 7:1–5 SKJV

		1		2		3		

Across

4. The ___ spoke to Noah (7:1)
5. Noah and all of his ____ were to go into the ark (7:1)
7. Everything _____ would be destroyed (7:4)
8. The Lord saw Noah as a ______ man (7:1)

Down

1. Noah did ____ to all the Lord commanded (7:5)
2. Both ___ and female animals were to be included (7:2)
3. It would rain for ____ days and nights (7:4)
6. "Of every clean _____ you shall take with you by sevens" (7:2)

COLORING PAGE

10. Noah and the Rainbow

DECODER

11. God's Promise to Noah

GENESIS 8:22 SKJV

	1	2	3	4	5
1	Q	Z	S	L	F
2	V	T	O	M	Y
3	X	D	A	P	R
4	I	G	N	H	J
5	B	W	C	U	E

"52–44–41–14–55 22–44–55 55–33–35–22–44
35–55–24–33–41–43–13, 13–55–55–32–22–41–24–55 33–43–32
44–33–35–21–55–13–22, 33–43–32 53–23–14–32 33–43–32
44–55–33–22, 33–43–32 13–54–24–24–55–35 33–43–32
52–41–43–22–55–35, 33–43–32 32–33–25 33–43–32
43–41–42–44–22 13–44–33–14–14 43–23–22 53–55–33–13–55."

ACROSTIC

12. At a Place Called Babel

GENESIS 11:1–9 NLV

"Now the ____ earth used the same language" (11:1) 34–11–27–9–42

"Men. . .____ a valley" (11:2) 6–25–17–44–31

"Let us make ____ and burn them" (11:3) 10–38–3–41–22–37

What the people wanted to build (11:4) 13–19–2–36

The _____ wanted to build a tower (11:4) 39–16–14–32–45–7

"Come, let Us go down and __ up their language" (11:7) 28–15–46

They could not _______ each other (11:7) 33–40–8–12–43–4–26–18–23–29

"They stopped ______ the city" (11:8) 5–20–47–21–30–1–35–24

37–27 26–11–16 44–18–28–42 14–6 2–11–7 13–47–26–36

34–18–37 5–18–10–42–38, 10–7–13–18–20–37–12 26–11–7–43–42

26–11–7 21–14–43–31 28–47–46–7–31 20–32 2–11–16

21–18–44–24–33–18–24–7 25–6 2–11–16 34–11–25–21–16

7–18–43–2–11.

CROSSWORD

13. Abram's New Name

Genesis 17:1–6 NLV

Across

3. "Your name will be ______" (17:5)
5. "I will ___ My agreement between Me and you" (17:2)
7. "____ will come from you" (17:6)
8. Abram "was _____-nine years old" when God spoke to him (17:1)

Down

1. "Obey Me, and be without ____" (17:1)
2. "I will make ______ of you" (17:6)
4. "___ will come from you" (17:6)
6. "I will ___ you many children" (17:2)

DECODER

14. Joseph's New Coat

GENESIS 37:3 SKJV

	1	2	3	4	5
1	F	Q	M	D	K
2	O	A	T	W	H
3	J	V	G	Y	S
4	R	I	P	B	N
5	C	U	L	X	E

45–21–24   42–35–41–22–55–53   53–21–32–55–14

31–21–35–55–43–25   13–21–41–55   23–25–22–45   22–53–53

25–42–35   51–25–42–53–14–41–55–45,   44–55–51–22–52–35–55

25–55   24–22–35   23–25–55   35–21–45   21–11   25–42–35

21–53–14   22–33–55,   22–45–14   25–55   13–22–14–55   25–42–13

22   51–21–22–23   21–11   13–22–45–34   51–21–53–21–41–35.

MAZE

15. Find Baby Moses' Way to Pharaoh's Daughter

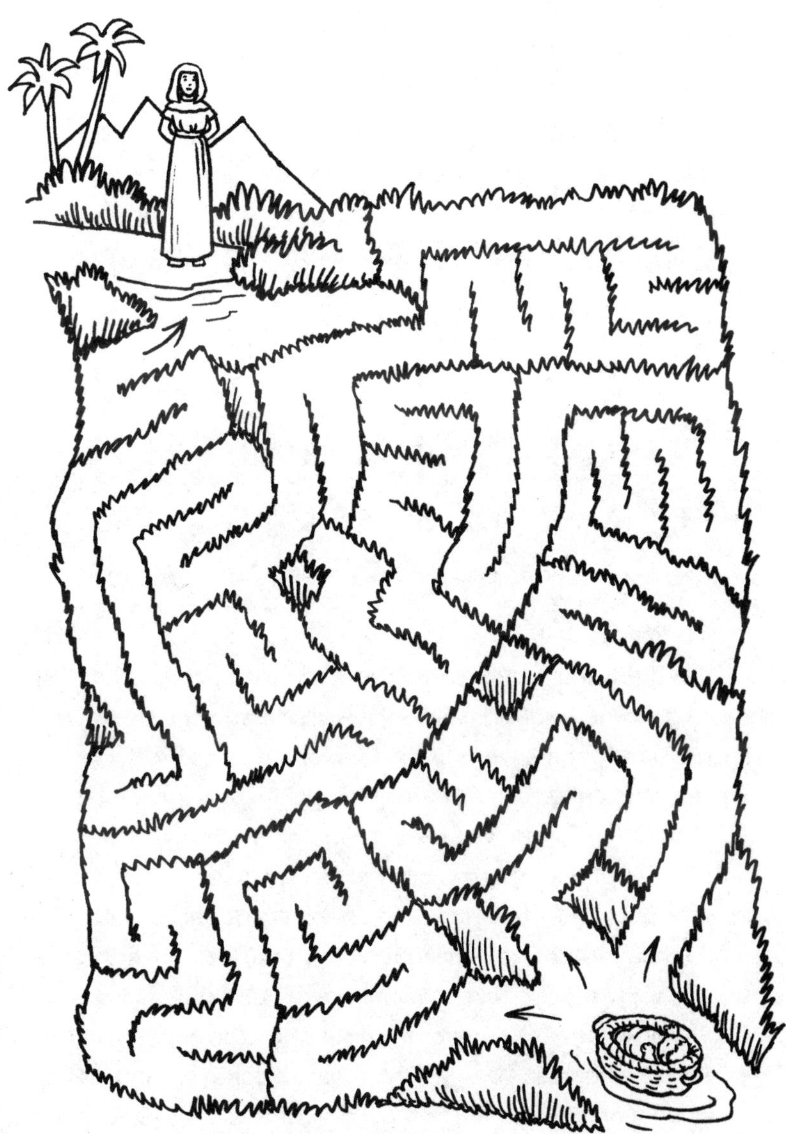

WORD SEARCH

16. Baby in a Basket

EXODUS 2:5–10 NLV

B	V	R	N	W	C	V	T	F	W
R	A	O	M	H	E	G	H	H	E
E	S	S	I	N	W	R	O	F	R
T	Z	L	K	W	X	A	B	W	G
H	D	H	P	E	R	S	K	E	T
G	R	D	K	A	T	S	M	L	H
U	E	F	H	N	I	L	E	H	R
A	T	P	E	S	R	U	N	D	K
D	A	M	O	S	E	S	B	P	R
F	W	W	B	Z	M	D	L	K	G

Then the **daughter** of **Pharaoh** came to wash herself in the **Nile**. Her young women walked beside the Nile. She saw the **basket** in the tall **grass** and sent the woman who served her to get it. She opened it and saw the **child**. The boy was crying. She had pity on him and said, "This is one of the Hebrews' children." Then his sister said to Pharaoh's daughter, "Should I go and call a **nurse** from the **Hebrew** women to nurse the child for you?" Pharaoh's daughter said to her, "Go." So the girl went and called the child's mother. Then Pharaoh's daughter said to her, "Take this child away and nurse him for me. And I will pay you." So the woman took the child and nursed him. The child **grew**, and she brought him to Pharaoh's daughter. And he became her **son**. She gave him the name **Moses**, saying, "Because I took him out of the **water**."

17. Plagues in Egypt

Exodus 7–11 NLV

Across

3. Green hoppers that covered Egypt (8:2)
6. "And there was ______ in all the land of Egypt for three days" (10:22)
8. "The Lord poured ___ on the land of Egypt" (9:23)
9. Moses tossed up ashes that "became ____ on man and animal" (9:10)

Down

1. "All the water in the Nile was turned into ____" (7:20)
2. Hungry, grasshopper-like bugs (10:4)
4. "And all the ____-born in the land of Egypt will die" (11:5)
5. "All the _____ of Egypt died" (9:6)
7. Disease-carrying bugs that filled Egypt (8:21)

DECODER

18. Parting the Sea

EXODUS 14:22 NLV

	1	2	3	4	5
1	D	U	I	O	B
2	K	G	S	N	Q
3	H	Y	E	V	J
4	P	L	X	C	T
5	A	R	M	W	F

51–24–11 45–31–33 41–33–14–41–42–33 14–55 13–23–52–51–33–42 54–33–24–45 45–31–52–14–12–22–31 45–31–33 23–33–51 14–24 11–52–32 42–51–24–11. 45–31–33 54–51–45–33–52–23 54–33–52–33 42–13–21–33 51 54–51–42–42 45–14 45–31–33–53 14–24 45–31–33–13–52 52–13–22–31–45 51–24–11 14–24 45–31–33–13–52 42–33–55–45.

ACROSTIC

19. Miriam's Song

EXODUS 15:19–21 NLV

Egypt's ruler whose horsemen went into the sea (15:19) — 4–11–7–23–18–21–29

The Israelites walked on ___ land (15:19) — 26–5–40

Miriam was a "woman who ____ for the Lord" (15:20) — 8–32–27–6–13

The women were ______ (15:20) — 9–24–31–1–22–3–28

The instrument being played (15:20) — 2–20–15–30–10–39–33

Miriam's brother's name was ____ (15:20) — 12–35–25–38–14

What the women did to Miriam (15:20) — 34–16–36–17–3–37–19–41

"8–22–14–28 2–21 2–29–13 33–21–5–9, 34–27–10 29–13

22–8 32–23–7–22–8–13–9 34–21–5 29–20–8

28–23–13–12–2–3–13–8–8."

COLORING PAGE

20. Moses and the Ten Commandments

WORD SEARCH

21. The Day of Rest

EXODUS 20:8–11 NLV

T	L	T	H	E	A	V	E	N	S
T	T	R	M	S	R	L	S	O	Y
R	N	A	P	T	E	X	N	I	N
E	A	V	S	W	R	A	F	M	X
B	V	E	E	H	O	L	Y	K	E
M	R	L	V	L	H	T	R	A	L
E	E	E	E	M	T	O	R	N	O
M	S	R	N	T	W	T	N	J	R
E	X	J	T	L	H	Y	A	O	D
R	E	T	H	G	U	A	D	C	R

"**Remember** the Day of **Rest**, to keep it **holy**. **Six** days you will do all your work. But the **seventh** day is a Day of Rest to the Lord your God. You, your **son**, your **daughter**, your male servant, your female **servant**, your **cattle**, or the **traveler** who stays with you, must not do any **work** on this day. For in six days the Lord made the **heavens**, the **earth**, the **sea** and all that is in them. And He rested on the seventh day. So the **Lord** gave **honor** to the Day of Rest and made it holy."

DECODER

22. The Lord in Cloud and Fire

Exodus 40:38 SKJV

	1	2	3	4	5
1	I	C	Q	N	G
2	P	T	E	W	J
3	V	F	L	D	S
4	B	Y	H	X	O
5	R	M	K	U	A

32–45–51 22–43–23 12–33–45–54–34 45–32 22–43–23

33–45–51–34 24–55–35 45–14 22–43–23

22–55–41–23–51–14–55–12–33–23 41–42 34–55–42, 55–14–34

32–11–51–23 24–55–35 45–14 11–22 41–42

14–11–15–43–22, 11–14 22–43–23 35–11–15–43–22 45–32

55–33–33 22–43–23 43–45–54–35–23 45–32

11–35–51–55–23–33, 22–43–51–45–54–15–43–45–54–22 55–33–33

22–43–23–11–51 25–45–54–51–14–23–42–35.

23. Water from a Rock

NUMBERS 20:6–9 SKJV

Moses was Aaron's _____ (20:6, 8)	6–18–23–11–3–20–1
"They fell on their ____" (20:6)	22–7–15–30–31
They saw the ____ of the Lord (20:6)	25–14–29–9–34
The Lord told Moses, "___ the rod" (20:7–8)	17–12–5–28
Moses and Aaron were to "gather the ______ together" (20:8)	27–4–16–19–2–10–24–32
The people and animals would be able to ____ (20:8)	13–33–21–8–26

7–8–13 2–29–16–28–4 17–23–29–5 17–3–19 9–23–13 22–1–23–2

6–28–22–23–18–20 17–3–28 14–23–1–13, 7–16 3–28

15–29–2–2–7–8–13–20–13 3–21–2.

WORD SEARCH

24. The Talking Donkey

NUMBERS 22:25–28 NLV

Q	Y	G	L	L	O	R	D	R	J
M	L	R	L	T	K	F	K	Q	C
A	F	F	G	C	T	O	E	K	T
A	W	K	I	N	L	O	E	R	K
L	R	T	M	E	A	T	R	N	Y
A	S	T	G	J	W	I	H	N	E
B	H	N	Z	M	G	A	T	T	K
V	A	X	M	H	X	N	L	F	N
P	R	L	T	F	E	L	T	L	O
T	H	K	F	M	O	U	T	H	D

The **donkey** saw the **angel** of the **Lord**. So she pushed herself against the **wall** and crushed Balaam's **foot** against it, so he hit her again. Then the angel of the Lord went farther. He stood in a narrow place where there was no way to turn to the **right** or the **left**. When the donkey saw the angel of the Lord, she lay down under **Balaam**. So Balaam was **angry** and hit the donkey with his **stick**. And the Lord opened the **mouth** of the donkey, and she said to Balaam, "What have I done to you? Why have you hit me these **three** times?"

COLORING PAGE

25. Balaam, His Donkey, and the Angel

ACROSTIC

26. Loving and Obeying God

DEUTERONOMY 6:4–9 NLV

Israel was commanded to ___ the Lord (6:5) 13–23–19–26

It was to be with their whole heart, ___, and strength (6:5) 20–6–12–1

"Keep these words in your ___" (6:6) 15–28–17–21–4

"Teach them to your ______" (6:7) 18–24–11–8–30–3–27–31

"Talk about them when you sit in your ___" (6:7) 29–9–14–7–25

The words were to be written on their ___ (6:9) 2–10–16–5–22

"15–5–10–3, 23 11–20–21–17–26–13! 16–15–25 13–9–21–30 6–12–21 2–23–30 11–20 23–31–5 8–23–21–30!"

CROSSWORD

27. Do Not Fear

DEUTERONOMY 31:7–8 SKJV

Across

2. Who Moses is speaking to (31:7)
4. "Be ____" (31:7)
6. God's special people (31:7)
8. "Be. . .of good ____" (31:7)

Down

1. "He will not fail you or ______ you" (31:8)
3. "Do not ____ or be dismayed" (31:8)
5. "He will be ____ you" (31:8)
7. "And the ____, it is He who goes before you" (31:8)

28. A Call for Courage

JOSHUA 1:9 NLV

	1	2	3	4	5
1	D	P	G	T	A
2	X	F	M	K	I
3	C	L	R	E	O
4	S	V	B	Q	W
5	H	N	Y	U	J

"51–15–42–34 25 52–35–14 14–35–32–11 53–35–54 ? 43–34

41–14–33–35–52–13 15–52–11 51–15–42–34

41–14–33–34–52–13–14–51 35–22 51–34–15–33–14 ! 11–35

52–35–14 43–34 15–22–33–15–25–11 35–33 32–35–41–34

22–15–25–14–51. 22–35–33 14–51–34 32–35–33–11

53–35–54–33 13–35–11 25–41 45–25–14–51 53–35–54

15–52–53–45–51–34–33–34 53–35–54 13–35."

29. Spying Out the Land

JOSHUA 2 NLV

Across

1. Woman the spies visited (2:1)
2. Number of spies sent into the land (2:1)
4. What Jericho felt about Israel (2:9)
5. What the spies climbed down from the woman's window (2:15)
7. Israelite leader who sent the spies (2:1)

Down

1. Where the woman hid the spies (2:6)
3. What the woman wanted Israel to do for her and her family (2:13, two words)
6. Where the woman's house sat (2:15)

COLORING PAGE

30. Joshua and the Battle of Jericho

WORD SEARCH

31. Instructions About Jericho

JOSHUA 6:2–5 SKJV

And the LORD said to **Joshua**, "See, I have given into your hand **Jericho**, and its **king**, and the mighty men of valor. And you shall **surround** the city, all you men of war, and go around the **city** once. You shall do this for **six** days. And seven priests shall bear seven **trumpets** of rams' horns before the ark, and the seventh day you shall surround the city **seven** times, and the **priests** shall blow with the trumpets. And it shall come to pass, that when they make a long blast with the ram's **horn**, and when you hear the sound of the trumpet, all the people shall **shout** with a great shout, and the **wall** of the city shall **fall** down flat, and the people shall ascend, every man straight before him."

CROSSWORD

32. Jericho Falls!

JOSHUA 6 KJV

Across

1. One sound that caused Jericho's wall to fall (6:20)
3. What Israel did to the city of Jericho (6:24)
5. Woman whose family was saved from death (6:25)
7. Valuable metal saved for the treasury of God's house (6:24)

Down

1. Weapon used against Jericho (6:21)
2. How Jericho's wall fell down (6:20)
4. Another sound that caused Jericho's wall to fall (6:20)
6. Another valuable metal saved for the treasury of God's house (6:24)

WORD SEARCH

33. The Sun Stands Still

JOSHUA 10:13–15 NLV

J	L	I	S	T	E	N	E	D	L
S	E	C	I	O	V	C	F	L	M
L	T	W	L	F	P	O	I	W	Z
M	O	O	N	K	U	T	H	R	T
N	M	G	P	G	S	O	F	M	K
A	W	K	H	P	L	T	T	C	D
T	Y	T	J	E	E	R	G	N	R
I	R	A	G	F	N	D	H	Z	O
O	P	M	D	D	U	Y	K	S	L
N	K	V	J	O	S	H	U	A	V

So the **sun** stood **still** and the **moon stopped**, until the **nation** punished those who **fought** against them. Is it not written in the Book of Jashar? The sun stopped in the center of the **sky**. It did not hurry to go down for about a **whole day**. There has been no day like it before or since, when the **Lord listened** to the **voice** of a man. For the Lord fought for Israel. Then **Joshua** and all Israel returned to the tents at Gilgal.

34. Joshua Chooses the Lord

JOSHUA 24:15 NLV

	1	2	3	4	5
1	C	S	K	E	R
2	V	J	B	M	O
3	N	A	U	Z	H
4	Y	W	I	D	X
5	G	T	L	F	P

"43–54 41–25–33 52–35–43–31–13 43–52 43–12

42–15–25–31–51 52–25 12–14–15–21–14 52–35–14 53–25–15–44,

11–35–25–25–12–14 52–25–44–32–41 42–35–25–24 41–25–33

42–43–53–53 12–14–15–21–14. . . . 23–33–52 32–12 54–25–15

24–14 32–31–44 24–41 54–32–24–43–53–41,

42–14 42–43–53–53 12–14–15–21–14 52–35–14 53–25–15–44."

COLORING PAGE

35. Samson and Delilah

ACROSTIC

36. Strong Man Samson

JUDGES 14–16 NLV/KJV

Samson killed this animal with his hands (14:5–6)	14–38–51–41
What Samson found inside of the animal later (14:8)	17–29–33–40–2
Samson caught three hundred of these (15:4)	45–6–24–19–37
What Samson set fire to (15:5 NLV)	4–15–47–39–44
Samson broke free from _____ (15:14 NLV)	30–10–5–22–49
Samson used the ______ of a donkey as a weapon (15:15)	13–31–35–48–8–21–46
What made Samson strong (16:17)	42–16–1–34
The people who ruled over Israel at this time (14:4)	12–27–43–32–3–36–28–20–7–25–23
Where the enemy's tents were (15:9)	26–18–11–50–9

47–7–11 17–40 26–18–11–4–40–11 43–23–30–16–40–14 1–7

28–17–46 11–47–2–36 51–45 28–42–40

12–17–39–14–1–37–28–39–33–22–37 28–35–46–41–28–2

2–40–47–15–36.

WORD SEARCH

37. Samson's Downfall

JUDGES 16:18–20 SKJV

And when **Delilah** saw that he had told her all his **heart**, she sent and called for the **lords** of the Philistines, saying, "Come up once more, for he has **shown** me all his heart." Then the lords of the Philistines came up to her and brought **money** in their hand. And she made him sleep on her knees, and she called for a man. And she had him **shave** off the **seven locks** of his head. And she began to afflict him, and his **strength** went from him. And she said, "The Philistines are upon you, **Samson**." And he **awoke** out of his sleep and said, "I will go out as before, at other times, and **shake** myself **free**." And he did not know that the LORD had **departed** from him.

CROSSWORD

38. Ruth's Hardship

RUTH 1 SKJV

Across

2. Ruth's sister-in-law's name (1:4)
5. Ruth's father-in-law's name (1:2–4)
7. How many years Ruth's mother-in-law Naomi lived outside Judah (1:4)
8. Where Ruth's husband died (1:4–5)

Down

1. "They came to Bethlehem in the beginning of barley _____" (1:22)
3. "Your _____ shall be my _____" (1:16, same word)
4. Town Naomi was from (1:2)
6. Naomi's new name (1:20)

WORD SEARCH

39. Bible Grains and Plants

Ruth harvested barley. Find these other grains and edible plants noted in the Bible.

Wheat (Exodus 34:22)
Spelt (Ezekiel 4:9)
Millet (Ezekiel 4:9)
Hyssop (John 19:29)
Garlic (Numbers 11:5)
Leeks (Numbers 11:5)
Onions (Numbers 11:5)
Coriander (Numbers 11:7)
Cucumbers (Isaiah 1:8)
Grapes (Revelation 14:18)
Mint (Matthew 23:23)

All names from the Simplified King James Version.

CONNECT THE DOTS

40. Ruth and Boaz

WORD SEARCH

41. A Basket of Barley

RUTH 2:17–19 NLV

K	V	L	M	Y	W	L	T	L	M
N	R	D	E	R	E	H	T	A	G
L	B	O	A	Z	Q	R	L	R	X
B	A	E	W	L	O	F	L	B	W
A	R	T	V	V	F	I	E	L	D
S	L	L	A	E	N	T	N	K	F
K	E	F	L	A	N	I	N	D	H
E	Y	Z	O	L	A	I	M	O	T
T	K	M	P	R	K	X	N	O	U
C	I	R	G	N	M	Y	N	G	R

So **Ruth** gathered **grain** in the **field** until **evening**. Then she beat out what she had gathered. It was enough **barley** to fill a **basket**. She picked it up and went into the city to show her mother-in-law what she had **gathered**. Ruth gave **Naomi** what she had left after she was filled. Her mother-in-law said to her, "Where did you gather grain today? Where did you **work**? May **good** come to the man who showed you **favor**." So Ruth told her mother-in-law, "The name of the man I worked with today is **Boaz**."

DECODER

42. Boaz and Ruth

Ruth 3:11 SKJV

	1	2	3	4	5
1	V	F	U	B	M
2	D	T	Q	L	G
3	Y	H	J	P	I
4	O	S	A	K	R
5	E	Z	N	W	C

"43–53–21 53–41–54, 15–31 21–43–13–25–32–22–51–45,

12–51–43–45 53–41–22. 35 54–35–24–24 21–41 12–41–45

31–41–13 43–24–24 22–32–43–22 31–41–13

45–51–23–13–35–45–51, 12–41–45 43–24–24 22–32–51

55–35–22–31 41–12 15–31 34–51–41–34–24–51 44–53–41–54

22–32–43–22 31–41–13 43–45–51 43 11–35–45–22–13–41–13–42

54–41–15–43–53."

DECODER

43. Hannah's Thanks to God

1 Samuel 2:2 SKJV

	1	2	3	4	5
1	I	C	R	M	H
2	S	O	U	F	D
3	L	G	J	Q	N
4	B	X	E	T	W
5	Y	K	V	P	A

44–15–43–13–43 11–21 35–22 22–35–43 15–22–31–51 31–11–52–43 44–15–43 31–22–13–25, 24–22–13 44–15–43–13–43 11–21 35–22 22–35–43 41–43–21–11–25–43–21 51–22–23, 35–22–13 11–21 44–15–43–13–43 55–35–51 13–22–12–52 31–11–52–43 22–23–13 32–22–25.

WORD SEARCH

44. God Calls to Samuel

1 SAMUEL 3:9–12 SKJV

E	A	R	S	X	H	Q	L	C	R
Z	E	D	R	O	L	E	X	W	N
S	N	V	U	C	A	L	L	S	S
B	P	S	E	R	M	H	G	N	E
S	E	E	S	R	E	M	L	D	R
P	D	I	A	A	Y	E	W	L	V
O	Z	O	R	K	U	O	J	O	A
K	L	S	O	M	H	I	N	H	N
E	X	W	A	T	R	L	Q	E	T
N	B	S	Q	T	S	E	T	B	J

Therefore **Eli** said to **Samuel**, "Go, lie down, and it shall be, if He **calls** you, that you shall say, '**Speak**, LORD, for Your **servant hears**.'" So Samuel went and lay down in his place. And the **LORD** came and **stood** and called as at other times, "Samuel, Samuel." Then Samuel answered, "Speak, for Your servant hears." And the LORD said to Samuel, "**Behold**, I will do a thing in **Israel** at which both the **ears** of **everyone** who hears it shall tingle. On that day I will perform against Eli all things that I have **spoken** concerning his **house**; when I begin, I will also make an end."

COLORING PAGE

45. Little Samuel

ACROSTIC

46. Israel's First King

1 Samuel 9–11; 13:1 NLV

"He was a ___ taller than any of the people" (9:2) 27–11–3–38

Saul was "a good-looking ____ man" (9:2) 30–44–13–36–41

Saul's dad's name (9:3) 16–7–39–47

Saul took a ______ with him to find the missing donkeys (9:3) 4–19–33–40–23–10–1

Saul went to find Samuel, the man __ God (9:18–19) 29–46

"Then _____ took a bottle of oil and poured it on Saul's head" (10:1) 49–6–22–32–17–21

"The donkeys you ___to look for have been found" (10:2) 26–9–45–34

God changed Saul's ____ (10:9) 15–8–24–42–35

Saul was "of the family group of _______" (10:20) 14–20–48–25–2–18–31–28

What Saul was found hiding among (10:22) 37–5–12–43

4–24–13–21 26–2–43 46–44–33–34–30 30–19–23–33–39

29–21–38 26–15–11–36 15–19 14–8–12–3–10 34–44 33–13–21–19.

47–17 42–32–21–11–38 44–40–19–42 31–43–33–24–8–21

1–15–31–33–1–30 - 34–26–29 30–8–5–33–49.

CROSSWORD

47. All About David

1 Samuel 13–18 SKJV

Across

2. David had a beautiful _____ (16:12)
4. David kept his father's _____ (17:34)
6. David's best friend (18:1)
8. The appearance of David's skin (16:12)

Down

1. David was one of the sons of _____ (16:19)
3. "And David. . .behaved _____" (18:5)
5. David was a man after God's own _____ (13:14)
7. The instrument David played (18:10)

DECODER

48. The Lord Sees the Heart

1 Samuel 16:7 NLV

	1	2	3	4	5
1	A	M	L	D	Q
2	X	H	V	Y	I
3	E	O	N	B	W
4	K	S	F	P	T
5	U	C	R	J	G

"43–32–53 45–22–31 13–32–53–14 14–32–31–42 33–32–45 13–32–32–41 11–45 45–22–31 45–22–25–33–55–42 12–11–33 13–32–32–41–42 11–45. 11 12–11–33 13–32–32–41–42 11–45 45–22–31 32–51–45–42–25–14–31 32–43 11 44–31–53–42–32–33, 34–51–45 45–22–31 13–32–53–14 13–32–32–41–42 11–45 45–22–31 22–31–11–53–45."

WORD SEARCH

49. Other Good Kings of the Bible

1–2 KINGS

N	M	L	A	W	B	T	Y	Z	X
O	Z	A	J	M	V	H	Z	P	P
M	K	R	H	Q	A	V	R	W	T
O	A	D	A	T	R	Z	J	N	L
L	Z	S	L	P	O	E	I	Y	C
O	A	X	K	N	H	J	X	A	L
S	R	Z	J	O	S	I	A	H	H
T	I	L	A	N	T	D	X	M	G
W	A	S	T	G	T	J	Q	D	R
P	H	H	A	I	K	E	Z	E	H

Asa (1 Kings 15:9–14)

Josiah (2 Kings 22:1–2)

Amaziah (2 Kings 14:1–3)

Azariah (2 Kings 15:1–4)

Jehoash (2 Kings 12:1–2)

Solomon (1 Kings 3:6–7)

Hezekiah (2 Kings 18:1–3)

Jotham (2 Kings 15:32–34)

All names from the Simplified King James Version.

COLORING PAGE

50. David and Goliath

ACROSTIC

51. A Giant Enemy

1 SAMUEL 17:4–7, 10 NLV

There was a man who was a "strong _____" (17:4) 18–33–5–43–29–11–21

His ___ was Goliath (17:4) 38–26–14–9

He came from the armies of the _______ (17:4) 20–31–24–36–7–40–37–3–16–30–13

"He was almost ____ as tall as most men" (17:4) 42–19–25–39–1

His ___ covering was made of brass (17:5) 28–44–6–35

He ___ brass battle-clothes that weighed around five thousand silver pieces (17:5) 12–46–27–8

The iron head of his spear weighed around six hundred pieces of ____ (17:7) 22–15–4–41–17–34

"A man walked before him to ____ his shield" (17:7) 2–23–10–32–45

23–5–26–24–16 29–31–1 20–43–3–4–15–22–37–25–38–11

40–26–24–35, "3 40–29–6–38–35 26–5–23–25–16–22–42

29–43–9 26–21–14–45 46–18 33–22–10–26–11–4 37–31–33–40

35–26–45. 5–15–41–1 14–44 6 14–23–16, 37–43–23–42 19–44

14–6–45 18–7–5–28–42 37–46–5–8–42–31–11–27."

DECODER

52. David's Warning for Goliath

1 Samuel 17:45 SKJV

	1	2	3	4	5
1	F	B	S	R	E
2	Z	L	Y	A	U
3	M	C	J	O	H
4	I	Q	T	P	D
5	N	W	G	V	K

43–35–15–51 45–24–54–41–45 13–24–41–45 43–34 43–35–15

44–35–41–22–41–13–43–41–51–15, "23–34–25 32–34–31–15 43–34

31–15 52–41–43–35 24 13–52–34–14–45 24–51–45 52–41–43–35

24 13–44–15–24–14 24–51–45 52–41–43–35 24

13–35–41–15–22–45. 12–25–43 41 32–34–31–15 43–34

23–34–25 41–51 43–35–15 51–24–31–15 34–11 43–35–15

22–34–14–45 34–11 35–34–13–43–13, 43–35–15 53–34–45

34–11 43–35–15 24–14–31–41–15–13 34–11 41–13–14–24–15–22,

52–35–34–31 23–34–25 35–24–54–15 45–15–11–41–15–45."

WORD SEARCH

53. David Defeats Goliath

1 SAMUEL 17:48–51 KJV

D	E	L	I	A	V	E	R	P	D
K	P	L	R	H	J	N	F	O	Q
G	D	C	G	G	V	I	O	Z	D
M	N	A	R	M	Y	T	S	S	A
H	G	I	F	N	S	S	H	T	E
K	A	E	L	D	K	I	E	O	H
Z	L	N	I	S	M	L	A	N	E
L	M	V	D	L	Z	I	T	E	R
T	A	G	R	H	H	H	H	L	O
D	S	W	O	R	D	P	Q	L	F

And it came to pass, when the **Philistine** arose, and came, and drew nigh to meet **David**, that David hastened, and ran toward the **army** to meet the Philistine. And David put his **hand** in his bag, and took thence a **stone**, and slang it, and smote the Philistine in his **forehead**, that the stone sunk into his forehead; and he **fell** upon his face to the earth. So David **prevailed** over the Philistine with a **sling** and with a stone, and smote the Philistine, and slew him; but there was no sword in the hand of David. Therefore David ran, and **stood** upon the Philistine, and took his **sword**, and drew it out of the **sheath** thereof, and slew him, and cut off his head therewith. And when the Philistines saw their champion was dead, they fled.

54. Celebrating David's Victory

1 SAMUEL 18:6–9 SKJV

Across

3. The women were playing "instruments of ____" (18:6)
4. Women were singing and _____ (18:6)
6. He was king at the time of David's victory (18:6)
8. The women sang that David had slain "____ thousands" (18:7)

Down

1. "The women came out of all cities of _____" (18:6)
2. Percussion instrument the women played (18:6)
5. The warrior David had defeated (17:23; 18:6)
7. How Israel's king felt about David's popularity (18:8)

COLORING PAGE

55. King David

CROSSWORD

56. Israel's Greatest King

2 SAMUEL 5:3–5 NLV

Across

3. "He ruled in ______ thirty-three years over all Israel and Judah" (5:5)
5. "He ruled over ____ seven years and six months" (5:5)
6. The nation's leaders met the new king in _____ (5:3)
7. He ruled for ____ years (5:4)

Down

1. The new king "made an agreement with them before the ___" (5:3)
2. "Then they chose ____ to be the king of Israel" (5:3)
4. He was "_____ years old when he became king" (5:4)

DECODER

57. David's Song

2 SAMUEL 22:2, 4 SKJV

	1	2	3	4	5
1	E	I	R	C	J
2	O	A	V	Y	G
3	H	Z	B	S	M
4	W	L	T	F	P
5	D	Q	N	K	U

43–31–11 42–21–13–51 12–34 35–24 13–21–14–54 22–53–51

35–24 44–21–13–43–13–11–34–34 22–53–51 35–24

51–11–42–12–23–11–13–11–13. . . . 12 41–12–42–42 14–22–42–42

21–53 43–31–11 42–21–13–51, 41–31–21 12–34 41–21–13–43–31–24

43–21 33–11 45–13–22–12–34–11–51, 34–21 12 34–31–22–42–42

33–11 34–22–23–11–51 44–13–21–35 35–24 11–53–11–35–12–11–34.

WORD SEARCH

58. Solomon Asks for Wisdom

1 Kings 3:7–9 NLV

E	C	N	E	R	E	F	F	I	D
B	A	D	C	C	R	I	R	R	T
D	A	V	I	D	N	V	G	C	N
Y	K	T	H	I	F	N	S	H	A
T	M	C	S	G	I	K	T	O	V
E	R	H	H	K	K	D	A	S	R
G	N	A	R	I	O	K	R	E	E
D	K	X	E	O	L	X	T	N	S
U	R	M	G	H	G	D	C	L	K
J	E	L	P	O	E	P	N	K	Q

"Now, O Lord my God, You have made Your **servant king** in place of my father **David**. But I am only a little **child**. I do not know how to **start** or **finish**. Your servant is among Your **people** which You have **chosen**. They are many people. There are too many people to number. So give Your servant an understanding **heart** to **judge** Your people and know the **difference** between **good** and **bad**. For who is able to judge Your many people?"

CROSSWORD

59. Building God's Temple

1 KINGS 5:2–6 SKJV

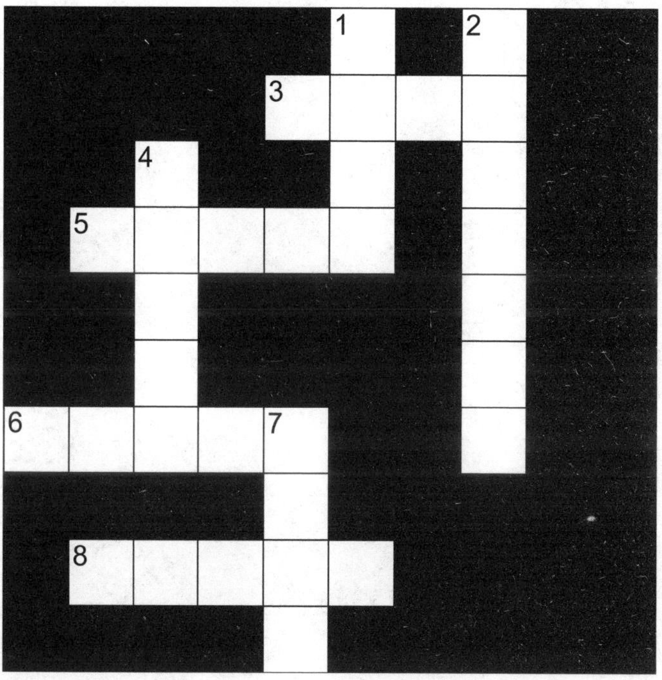

Across

3. Solomon wanted to build a place "for the ____ of the LORD" (5:5)
5. Solomon promised ______ for the servants who built the temple (5:6)
6. The kind of wood Solomon wanted for the temple (5:6)
8. Another name for the temple (5:5)

Down

1. They kept Solomon's father from building the temple (5:3)
2. Where the temple's wood came from (5:6)
4. Solomon's father, ____, could not build the temple (5:3)
7. Solomon had "_____ on every side" (5:4)

COLORING PAGE

60. Ravens Feed Elijah

DECODER

61. Elijah and the Ravens

1 Kings 17:2–4 NLV

	1	2	3	4	5
1	H	S	O	D	F
2	B	W	N	I	V
3	Q	L	E	R	K
4	J	Y	T	M	X
5	G	P	C	U	A

55–23–14 43–11–33 22–13–34–14 13–15 43–11–33 32–13–34–14

53–55–44–33 43–13 11–24–44, 12–55–42–24–23–51,

"32–33–55–25–33 11–33–34–33 55–23–14 43–54–34–23

33–55–12–43. 11–24–14–33 42–13–54–34–12–33–32–15 21–42

43–11–33 34–24–25–33–34 53–11–33–34–24–43–11, 33–55–12–43

13–15 43–11–33 41–13–34–14–55–23. 42–13–54 22–24–32–32

14–34–24–23–35 15–34–13–44 43–11–33 34–24–25–33–34.

55–23–14 24 11–55–25–33 43–13–32–14 43–11–33

34–55–25–33–23–12 43–13 21–34–24–23–51 15–13–13–14 43–13

42–13–54 43–11–33–34–33."

ACROSTIC

62. A Boy Comes Back to Life

1 Kings 17:17–22 NLV

"The son of the woman who owned the ____ became sick" (17:17) 22–10–35–6–29

The son became sick and "there was no ____ left in him" (17:17) 11–27–33–9–13–17

Who did the woman accuse at first? (17:18) 24–19–3–32–8–26

He said to her, "____ me your son" (17:19) 37–1–20–31

"Then he. . .____ him up to the room" (17:19) 21–7–14–34–5–36–18

"Have You brought trouble to the ____?" (17:20) 25–12–2–28–30

"Let this child's ____ return to him" (17:21) 15–4–23–16

13–26–29 15–12–34–18 22–31–7–27–18 13–26–16

20–12–4–21–29 10–23 16–15–1–32–28–22. 9–30–18 13–26–31

19–5–23–29 10–23 13–26–33 21–26–4–19–18

14–16–13–35–27–30–33–18 13–12 26–5–2 7–30–18 26–31

11–36–21–8–2–24 6–13–34–10–30–37 8–37–9–1–30.

ACROSTIC

63. Elijah on Mount Carmel

1 Kings 18:36–39 SKJV

The time of day for the sacrifice (18:36) 9–37–21–14–40–27–33

Elijah was a _____ (18:36) 18–4–35–10–31–42–16

What Elijah did to the Lord (18:36) 22–6–24–32–11–41

"You have _____ their hearts back again" (18:37) 12–25–19–8–43–29

"Then the fire of the Lord ___" (18:38) 38–1–17–30

The fire _____ the burnt sacrifice, wood, stones, and dust (18:38) 20–3–23–15–26–7–34–39

The fire also licked up the ____ (18:38) 13–5–36–28–2

24–14–41 13–31–43–14 5–30–17 16–31–34 10–42–35–18–17–28 15–24–13 40–12, 16–31–1–32 38–11–30–17 35–14 16–31–34–40–4 38–5–20–43–15. 24–8–41 16–31–21–32 15–24–40–29, "12–31–9 17–35–19–39, 31–11 40–15 33–35–29; 16–31–21 30–35–6–41, 31–21 40–15 33–3–41."

64. Nehemiah and the King

NEHEMIAH 2:5 NLV

	1	2	3	4	5
1	D	V	I	N	A
2	K	Y	G	Q	F
3	P	M	R	H	T
4	E	J	U	L	W
5	C	S	O	Z	B

15–14–11 13 52–15–13–11 35–53 35–34–41 21–13–14–23, "13–25 13–35 31–44–41–15–52–41–52 35–34–41 21–13–14–23, 15–14–11 13–25 22–53–43–33 52–41–33–12–15–14–35 34–15–52 25–53–43–14–11 25–15–12–53–33 13–14 22–53–43–33 41–22–41–52, 52–41–14–11 32–41 35–53 42–43–11–15–34, 35–53 35–34–41 51–13–35–22 53–25 32–22 25–15–35–34–41–33–52' 23–33–15–12–41–52. 44–41–35 32–41 55–43–13–44–11 13–35 15–23–15–13–14."

WHAT DOESN'T BELONG?

65. Nehemiah Rebuilds the Walls of Jerusalem

CROSSWORD

66. Celebrating the Wall

NEHEMIAH 12:27, 43 NLV

Across

3. God had given the people ____ joy (12:43)
4. "Timbrels and ____ were played" (12:27)
6. The people sang songs of _____ (12:27)
7. Even the ____ and children were filled with joy (12:43)

Down

1. The people looked for these temple workers (12:27)
2. The people praised God for the wall of _______ (12:27)
3. The people gave "many good ____" (12:43)
5. The people's joy "was heard from ___ ___" (12:43, two words)

CROSSWORD

67. Mordecai and Esther

ESTHER 2:5–7 NLV

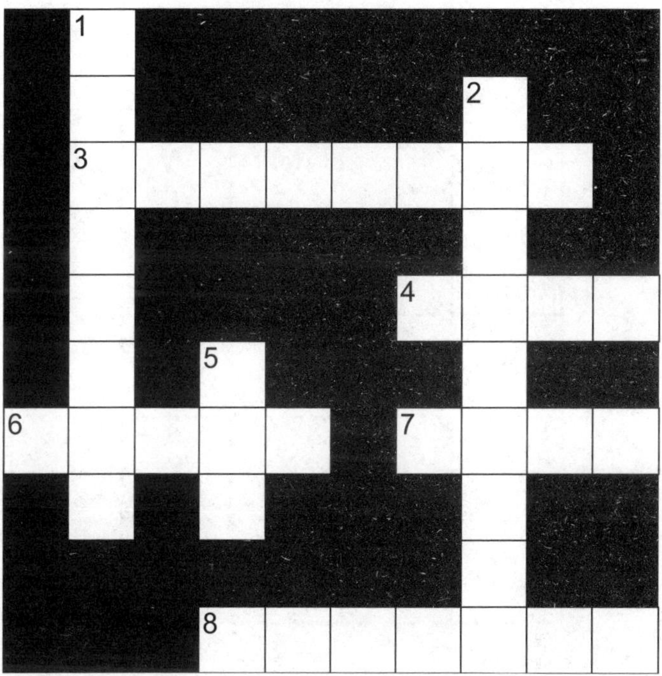

Across

3. Mordecai took Esther as his own ______ (2:7)
4. The city where the Persian king lived (2:5)
6. Mordecai "had been ____ from Jerusalem" (2:6)
7. Mordecai's great-grandfather (2:5)
8. Nebuchadnezzar was the king of ______ (2:6)

Down

1. Another name for Esther (2:7)
2. "The young lady was _______ in body and face" (2:7)
5. "There was a ___ whose name was Mordecai" (2:5)

DECODER

68. A Bold Request

ESTHER 7:3 NLV

	1	2	3	4	5
1	A	T	M	W	G
2	Q	H	B	P	K
3	E	Y	O	F	S
4	J	C	X	L	U
5	N	I	V	R	D

21–45–31–31–51 31–35–12–22–31–54 11–51–35–14–31–54–31–55,

"52–34 52 22–11–53–31 34–33–45–51–55 34–11–53–33–54

52–51 32–33–45–54 31–32–31–35, 33 25–52–51–15. . .52

11–35–25 12–22–11–12 13–32 44–52–34–31 11–51–55 12–22–31

44–52–53–31–35 33–34 13–32 24–31–33–24–44–31 23–31

35–11–53–31–55."

WORD SEARCH

69. The Jews Celebrate

ESTHER 8:15–17 SKJV

D	I	R	J	T	S	A	E	F	E
E	A	D	F	G	N	D	G	M	L
C	C	D	L	O	G	N	J	W	P
R	E	M	V	B	I	L	O	H	R
E	D	L	N	K	L	L	Y	I	U
E	R	K	K	E	Z	U	C	T	P
R	O	Y	A	L	N	R	E	E	H
R	M	S	F	V	O	I	M	M	Z
J	U	N	V	W	D	W	L	K	X
S	T	Q	N	H	O	N	O	R	N

And **Mordecai** went out from the presence of the **king** in **royal** apparel of **blue** and **white**, and with a great **crown** of **gold**, and with a garment of fine **linen** and **purple**. And the city of **Susa** rejoiced and was glad. The Jews had light, gladness, joy, and **honor**. And in every province and in every city, wherever the king's commandment and his **decree** came, the Jews had **joy** and gladness, a **feast**, and a good day. And many of the people of the land became Jews, for the fear of the Jews fell on them.

FINISH THE PICTURE

70. Queen Esther

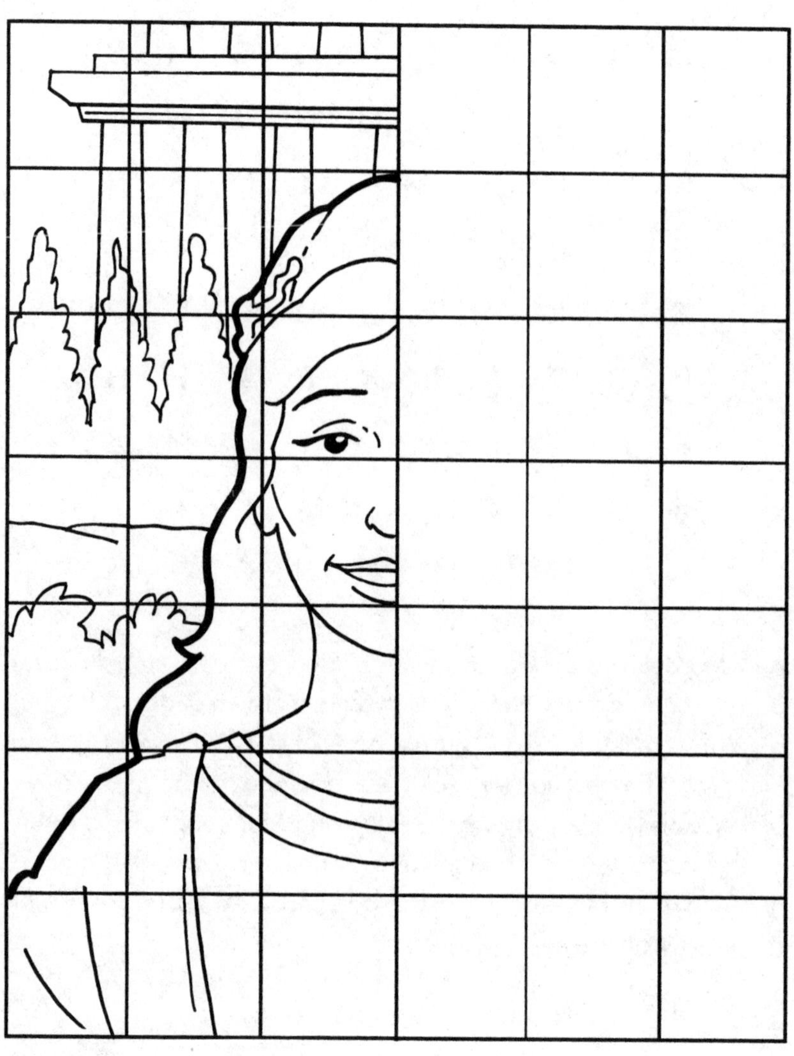

WORD SEARCH

71. You Are Unique. . .and Loved

PSALM 139:13–18 NLV

Q	N	R	E	B	M	U	N	B	R
C	W	B	D	W	D	T	O	J	J
G	R	V	I	T	N	N	R	M	S
R	I	S	S	M	E	E	A	T	N
E	T	E	N	S	H	P	H	S	A
A	T	Y	I	T	M	G	E	W	Y
T	E	E	E	S	U	A	A	E	N
N	N	G	Y	O	M	K	D	R	D
N	O	A	H	T	E	R	C	E	S
T	D	T	T	H	A	N	K	S	N

For You made the parts **inside** me. You put me **together** inside my mother. I will give **thanks** to You, for the greatness of the way I was **made** brings fear. Your works are **great** and my soul knows it very well. My **bones** were not hidden from You when I was made in **secret** and put together with care in the **deep** part of the earth. Your **eyes** saw me before I was put together. And all the **days** of my life were **written** in Your book before any of them came to be. Your **thoughts** are of great worth to me, O God. How many there are! If I could **number** them, there would be more than the **sand**. When I **awake**, I am still with You.

DECODER

72. Trust God's Way

Proverbs 3:5–6 SKJV

	1	2	3	4	5
1	F	R	M	U	C
2	H	Y	A	E	J
3	T	D	X	L	O
4	K	V	G	P	S
5	I	N	W	Q	B

31–12–14–45–31 51–52 31–21–24 34–35–12–32 53–51–31–21

23–34–34 22–35–14–12 21–24–23–12–31 23–52–32 32–35

52–35–31 34–24–23–52 35–52 22–35–14–12 35–53–52

14–52–32–24–12–45–31–23–52–32–51–52–43. 51–52 23–34–34

22–35–14–12 53–23–22–45 23–15–41–52–35–53–34–24–32–43–24

21–51–13, 23–52–32 21–24 45–21–23–34–34 32–51–12–24–15–31

22–35–14–12 44–23–31–21–45.

73. Strength for the Weary

Isaiah 40:29–31 SKJV

Across

2. "They shall mount up with wings like _____" (40:31)
3. "But those who wait on the LORD shall _____ their strength" (40:31)
5. "And the young men shall utterly _____ " (40:30)
7. "He increases the _____ of those who have no might" (40:29)

Down

1. "Even the youths shall faint and be _____ " (40:30)
4. "And they shall ____ and not faint" (40:31)
5. "He gives power to the _____" (40:29)
6. "They shall ____ and not be weary" (40:31)

DECODER

74. Jeremiah's Calling

JEREMIAH 1:4–5 NLV

	1	2	3	4	5
1	I	F	U	P	C
2	M	V	H	S	L
3	B	K	O	X	E
4	R	Y	D	T	Q
5	G	N	W	J	A

52–33–53 44–23–35 53–33–41–43 33–12 44–23–35

25–33–41–43 15–55–21–35 44–33 21–35 24–55–42–11–52–51,

"31–35–12–33–41–35 11 24–44–55–41–44–35–43 44–33

14–13–44 42–33–13 44–33–51–35–44–23–35–41 11–52

42–33–13–41 21–33–44–23–35–41, 11 32–52–35–53 42–33–13.

31–35–12–33–41–35 42–33–13 53–35–41–35 31–33–41–52, 11

24–35–44 42–33–13 55–14–55–41–44 55–24 23–33–25–42."

COLORING PAGE

75. Shadrach, Meshach, and Abednego

ACROSTIC

76. Worship Only God

DANIEL 3:14–18 KJV

The boys' names were Shadrach, _____, and Abednego (3:14) 23–14–31–11–2–37–27

They did not want to _____ the golden image (3:14) 16–7–33–25–39–13–29

The penalty of disobedience was a _____ fiery furnace (3:15) 9–21–12–34–30–5–28

One of the instruments that would play was the ____ (3:15) 17–22–1–35–19

Nebuchadnezzar was the ____ (3:16) 6–32–24–4

The boys said, "Our God whom we serve is able to _____ us" (3:17) 15–26–18–36–41–3–40

"We will not serve ___ gods" (3:18) 38–20–10

9–1–38 13–17 34–7–35, 9–3 32–35 6–34–7–16–5 21–24–35–7

35–27–3–26, 7 6–30–5–4, 35–11–2–35 16–19 16–32–22–18

34–7–35 25–14–33–41–19 38–27–10 28–7–15–25, 24–7–12

16–7–40–31–20–30–29 35–20–3 28–7–18–15–14–5 30–23–2–28–26

16–27–13–37–39 35–20–7–1 11–2–25–35 31–26–38 21–29.

WORD SEARCH

77. Daniel and the Lions

DANIEL 6:19–23 NLV

G R S H T U O M E D

N L H U R R Y S V E

I N I N V W I L D S

K E F O L R T E H A

M V W Q N D T L O E

M A K U A S E T L L

G S S N U G Y D E P

Y R I R N E C I O V

D E T A Q S H U T G

L Y K G N I V I L X

The **king** got up at **sunrise** and went in a **hurry** to the place where **lions** were kept. When he came to the **hole** in the ground where **Daniel** was, he called to him with a troubled **voice**, "Daniel, servant of the **living** God, has your **God**, Whom you always serve, been able to **save** you from the lions?" Then Daniel said to the king, "O king, live forever! My God sent His **angel** and **shut** the lions' **mouths**. They have not hurt me, because He knows that I am not guilty, and because I have done nothing wrong to you, O king." Then the king was very **pleased** and had Daniel taken up out of the hole in the ground. So they took Daniel out of the hole and saw that he had not been hurt at all, because he had **trusted** in his God.

DECODER

78. God's Desire

Hosea 6:6 KJV

	1	2	3	4	5
1	F	R	B	Q	J
2	T	O	X	P	D
3	S	H	L	E	U
4	A	V	N	I	M
5	K	C	Y	W	G

11–22–12 44 25–34–31–44–12–34–25 45–34–12–52–53, 41–43–25 43–22–21 31–41–52–12–44–11–44–52–34; 41–43–25 21–32–34 51–43–22–54–33–34–25–55–34 22–11 55–22–25 45–22–12–34 21–32–41–43 13–35–12–43–21 22–11–11–34–12–44–43–55–31.

CROSSWORD

79. Seeking Good

AMOS 5:14–15 SKJV

Across

4. "Seek ____" (5:14)
5. "Hate the ____" (5:15)
7. "The LORD, the God of ____, shall be with you" (5:14)
8. Another name for Israel (5:15)

Down

1. "Establish ______" (5:15)
2. How God may be to the obedient (5:15)
3. "____ the good" (5:15)
6. When you seek good, you may ____ (5:14)

COLORING PAGE

80. Jonah and the Big Fish

ACROSTIC

81. Jonah Disobeys God

JONAH 1:4–9 NLV

The wind was ______ (1:4) 17–5–24–37–2–22–28–9

The ______ were afraid (1:5) 23–30–8–26–7–13–20

"Every man cried to his ____" (1:5) 42–21–3

Things were tossed overboard so the ship wouldn't be as _____ (1:5) 4–12–18–33–29

Who was sleeping below deck? (1:5) 40–25–15–1–32

The _____ asked him, "How can you sleep?" (1:6) 35–41–10–27–11–39–19

"They ____ names, and Jonah's name was drawn" (1:7) 36–31–16–43

The sailors asked, "Who is to ___ for this?" (1:8) 43–14–34–6–38

40–5–19–30–32 20–34–8–36 27–25 27–32–37–6, "8 18–6 30 4–16–43–31–12–24, 18–15–36 39 24–7–2–20–4–39–17 27–4–38 9–25–31–36 42–25–36 7–22 4–38–30–33–37–15 24–4–25 6–11–36–12 27–32–38 20–37–18 1–19–36 27–32–12 36–13–29 9–34–15–36."

DECODER

82. Fish Swallows Man!

JONAH 1:17 SKJV

	1	2	3	4	5
1	B	W	E	S	H
2	R	A	Y	K	O
3	M	X	G	N	C
4	D	J	Q	V	T
5	I	P	U	L	F

34–25–12 45–15–13 54–25–21–41 15–22–41

52–21–13–52–22–21–13–41 22 33–21–13–22–45 55–51–14–15

45–25 14–12–22–54–54–25–12 42–25–34–22–15. 22–34–41

42–25–34–22–15 12–22–14 51–34 45–15–13 11–13–54–54–23

25–55 45–15–13 55–51–14–15 45–15–21–13–13 41–22–23–14

22–34–41 45–15–21–13–13 34–51–33–15–45–14.

WORD SEARCH

83. Living Creatures of the Bible

W	O	R	R	A	P	S	K	Y	R
R	B	L	R	W	C	N	P	L	M
P	E	W	Z	A	P	E	G	Q	P
T	E	O	M	J	E	A	J	H	C
N	T	E	R	H	L	G	X	R	Q
J	L	C	S	A	W	L	A	R	N
R	E	T	P	M	V	E	U	H	O
L	H	R	A	M	B	E	C	B	I
K	Z	D	R	A	G	O	N	T	L
E	S	R	O	H	L	P	L	J	N

Many living creatures are mentioned in the Bible. See if you can find these!

Lion (1 Peter 5:8)
Sheep (Matthew 9:36)
Ram (Genesis 22:13)
Raven (Genesis 8:7)
Eagle (Deuteronomy 14:12)
Camel (Matthew 19:24)
Sparrow (Psalm 102:7)
Bull (Isaiah 65:25)
Owl (Isaiah 34:14)
Horse (Jeremiah 8:6)
Bear (Lamentations 3:10)
Dragon (Psalm 91:13)
Beetle (Leviticus 11:22)

All names from the Simplified King James Version.

ACROSTIC

84. Prayer from a Dark Place

JONAH 2:1–10 NLV/SKJV

The man who spoke the words of this prayer (2:1) 8–25–37–43–20

He _____ from a fish's belly (2:1) 27–31–4–19–33–41

"The _____ surrounded me" (2:3 SKJV) 40–11–9–22–14–36

He looked toward God's holy _____ (2:4 SKJV) 44–6–38–13–23–1

His ____ fainted within him (2:7 SKJV) 12–42–30–5

He worshipped with a ______ voice (2:9 NLV) 39–10–3–24–17–34–29–16

"_______ is of the LORD" (2:9 SKJV) 26–2–18–35–7–28–21–32–15

4–15–14 28–10–6 11–42–31–41 26–27–9–17–1 39–25 44–10–33 40–21–36–20, 3–15–14 21–28 35–32–38–21–39–33–14 25–29–28 8–22–24–7–10 9–15 39–20–1 14–31–19 5–4–24–14.

MAZE

85. Jonah Runs from God

DECODER

86. How to Live

MICAH 6:8 SKJV

	1	2	3	4	5
1	L	A	P	V	C
2	Y	T	D	I	N
3	G	O	W	B	K
4	S	U	M	H	Q
5	F	J	R	E	X

44–54 44–12–41 41–44–32–33–25 21–32–42, 32 43–12–25,

33–44–12–22 24–41 31–32–32–23. 12–25–23 33–44–12–22

23–32–54–41 22–44–54 11–32–53–23 53–54–45–42–24–53–54

32–51 21–32–42, 34–42–22 22–32 12–15–22 52–42–41–22–11–21

12–25–23 22–32 11–32–14–54 43–54–53–15–21 12–25–23 22–32

33–12–11–35 44–42–43–34–11–21 33–24–22–44 21–32–42–53

31–32–23?

DECODER

87. Our Safe Place

Nahum 1:7 NLV

	1	2	3	4	5
1	B	R	M	H	I
2	F	J	U	Y	A
3	K	V	C	E	X
4	P	L	O	W	T
5	G	Q	S	N	D

45–14–34 42–43–12–55 15–53 51–43–43–55, 25

53–25–21–34 41–42–25–33–34 15–54 45–15–13–34–53

43–21 45–12–43–23–11–42–34. 25–54–55 14–34

31–54–43–44–53 45–14–43 53–34 44–14–43 33–43–13–34

45–43 14–15–13 45–43 11–34 53–25–21–34.

CROSSWORD

88. Joy in the Lord

Habakkuk 3:17–19 NLV

Across

4. "The Lord God is my ______" (3:19)
5. "The ____ give no food" (3:17)
7. "Even if the _____ do not grow" (3:17)

Down

1. "Even if there are no _____ within the fence" (3:17)
2. "No ____ in the ____-building" (3:17, same word)
3. "Even if the fig tree does not grow ____" (3:17)
4. "I will be glad in the God Who ____ me" (3:18)
5. "And there is no ____ on the vines" (3:17)
6. "Yet I will have ____ in the Lord" (3:18)

CROSSWORD

89. Jesus Is Born

LUKE 2:4–7 KJV

Across

1. Mary gave birth to her firstborn ___ (2:7)
4. The new parents laid the baby in a _____ (2:7)
5. Joseph was of the lineage of ____ (2:4)
7. Joseph left this city in Galilee (2:4)

Down

1. The baby was wrapped in _______ clothes (2:7)
2. "There was no room for them in the _____" (2:7)
3. The city of David is also called _______ (2:4)
6. Mary was "____ with child" (2:5)

COLORING PAGE

90. Christmas Visitors

ACROSTIC

91. Wise Men Visit Jesus

MATTHEW 2:7–12 SKJV

Herod "____ called the wise men" (2:7) 7–34–20–40–16–31–24–11

He asked them when the ___ had appeared (2:7) 12–38–18–22

Herod sent them to _______ (2:8) 39–17–6–25–14–33–8–29–3

The king said he wanted to _____ the baby (2:8) 26–13–5–41–19–32–10

The star they saw in the ___ led them (2:9) 28–9–35–2

"They saw the ____ Child with Mary, His mother" (2:11) 15–37–27–1–23

"They presented gifts to Him: ___, and frankincense, and myrrh" (2:11) 36–4–21–30

18–1–30 39–34–32–1–36 26–9–5–1–16–30 39–15 36–13–30

32–1 18 30–22–28–18–3 31–25–9–6 2–19–29–11

41–8–13–27–24–30 1–13–6 40–17–6–27–5–1 31–4 19–28–22–13–30,

6–19–28–15 30–16–10–18–40–6–17–30 2–37 31–25–29–32–22

13–26–1 20–37–27–1–6–5–11 9–1–13–31–8–16–5 26–9–15.

ACROSTIC

92. Be Salt and Light

MATTHEW 5:13–16 NLV

"You are the salt of the ____" (5:13) 33–18–24–11–3

___ that loses its taste is worthless (5:13) 30–17–4–9

Salt that isn't good anymore is thrown ____ (5:13) 22–31–6–14

"You are the light ___ the world" (5:14) 5–28

There is no way to hide a city on a ______ (5:14) 26–19–1–29–16–10–21–7

A lamp should not be put ____ a basket (5:15) 27–8–20–13–25

The lamp should be on a table so it ____ light (5:15) 23–12–32–15–2

"4–15–16 14–19–27–24 4–12–23–3–11 30–3–21–8–15 12–7

28–25–19–7–9 19–28 26–15–8. 16–3–33–8 11–3–13–14

31–21–4–4 30–33–13 16–3–13 23–5–19–20 16–3–12–8–23–30

14–19–27 20–5 17–29–20 31–21–4–4 3–5–7–5–25 14–5–1–24

28–10–16–3–13–24 31–3–19 21–2 12–8 3–13–18–32–13–8."

DECODER

93. The Golden Rule

MATTHEW 7:12 SKJV

	1	2	3	4	5
1	I	V	O	B	R
2	G	P	X	N	Y
3	K	S	E	W	F
4	Q	H	U	C	L
5	A	M	J	T	D

"54–42–33–15–33–35–13–15–33, 11–24 51–45–45

54–42–11–24–21–32, 34–42–51–54–33–12–33–15 25–13–43

34–51–24–54 52–33–24 54–13 55–13 54–13 25–13–43, 55–13

33–12–33–24 32–13 54–13 54–42–33–52,

35–13–15 54–42–11–32 11–32 54–42–33 45–51–34 51–24–55

54–42–33 22–15–13–22–42–33–54–32."

ACROSTIC

94. Jesus Is Baptized

JOHN 1:29–34 NLV

____ the Baptist saw Jesus coming (1:29) 9–35–14–40

"See! The Lamb of God Who takes away
the sin of the ____!" (1:29) 17–29–6–43–38

"One is coming after me Who is
more ______ than I" (1:30) 4–21–10–32–8–25–34–7–12

"He lived ____ I was born" (1:30) 39–28–16–44–20–27

"I have come. . .so the Jews might
know ____ Him" (1:31) 11–31–3–24–19

"I saw the ___ Spirit come down" (1:32) 30–2–42–23

"___ sent me to baptize with water" (1:33) 33–5–26

"He is the One Who _____ with the
Holy Spirit" (1:33) 15–1–36–13–22–41–37–18

"4 18–11–17 13–14–4–18 30–1–10–36–37–40. 22 34–21 7–29–17 18–11–23–22–40–33 13–30–34–25 9–37–18–24–18 4–18 25–30–37 18–5–40 2–16 33–32–38."

COLORING PAGE

95. Jesus' Baptism

WORD SEARCH

96. Sweet Freedom

ROMANS 8:3–5 SKJV

L	F	U	L	F	I	L	L	E	D
F	I	X	T	K	M	Z	C	S	S
S	C	K	A	I	T	M	G	L	I
Z	G	E	E	C	R	N	Y	W	N
K	W	N	M	N	I	I	A	R	F
N	G	W	I	H	E	L	P	M	U
I	J	A	T	H	K	S	Z	S	L
H	Z	L	Z	D	T	R	S	M	T
T	D	E	N	M	E	D	N	O	C
N	Z	F	L	E	S	H	R	Q	L

For what the **law** could not do, in that it was **weak** through the **flesh**, God did by sending His own Son in the **likeness** of **sinful** flesh and for sin: He **condemned** sin in the flesh, that the righteousness of the law might be **fulfilled** in us who **walk** not according to the flesh but according to the **Spirit**. For those who are according to the flesh **think** about the **things** of the flesh, but those who are according to the Spirit, the things of the Spirit.

CROSSWORD

97. True Love

1 Corinthians 13:4–8 NLV

Across

3. "Love does not get ____" (13:5)
5. "Love is ___" (13:4)
6. "Love ____ for all things" (13:7)
8. "Love _____ all things" (13:7)
9. "Love never comes to an __" (13:8)

Down

1. "Love is not _____" (13:4)
2. "Love is happy with the ____" (13:6)
4. "Love does not ___ up" (13:4)
7. "Love has no ____" (13:4)

WORD SEARCH

98. What to Think About

PHILIPPIANS 4:8 KJV

K	N	Y	T	H	I	N	G	S	R
M	E	R	L	J	F	T	M	E	B
N	R	R	M	E	R	F	V	D	M
H	H	B	P	O	V	E	Q	O	M
O	T	T	P	R	O	O	J	O	R
N	E	E	R	S	A	U	L	G	L
E	R	Y	T	U	S	I	L	T	T
S	B	A	L	T	E	X	S	J	K
T	H	V	I	R	T	U	E	E	N
W	M	H	E	R	U	P	B	F	T

Finally, **brethren**, **whatsoever things** are **true**, whatsoever things are **honest**, whatsoever things are **just**, whatsoever things are **pure**, whatsoever things are **lovely**, whatsoever things are of **good report**; if there be any **virtue**, and if there be any **praise**, think on these things.

ACROSTIC

99. Saul's Change of Heart

Acts 9:17–20 SKJV

Who helped Saul? (9:17) 24–17–44–6–32–20–39

Who appeared to Saul on the road? (9:17) 14–29–42–19–37

Saul was filled with the ____ Spirit (9:17) 47–8–16–22

Something like scales ____ from Saul's eyes (9:18) 38–11–2–31

Saul received his sight and
was ______ (9:18) 33–9–41–21–13–26–35–10

Saul was _________ when
he ate food (9:19) 36–12–23–43–7–15–34–1–27–45–3–48

What town was Saul in? (9:19) 5–28–40–18–46–25–4–30

20–7–10 32–40–40–35–5–13–24–21–3–16–22 1–29

41–23–11–9–25–47–35–48 25–1–23–32–39–21 13–6 12–47–11

42–22–45–44–15–8–15–19–27–30.

COLORING PAGE

100. Saul Is Saved

COLORING PAGE

101. Jesus Loves You!

ANSWERS

ACROSTIC

1. God's First Creation

NOTHING / WATERS /
SEEDS / BIRDS / MALE

Then God said, "Let there be light," and there was light.

GENESIS 1:3 NLV

WORD SEARCH

2. God Creates Humans

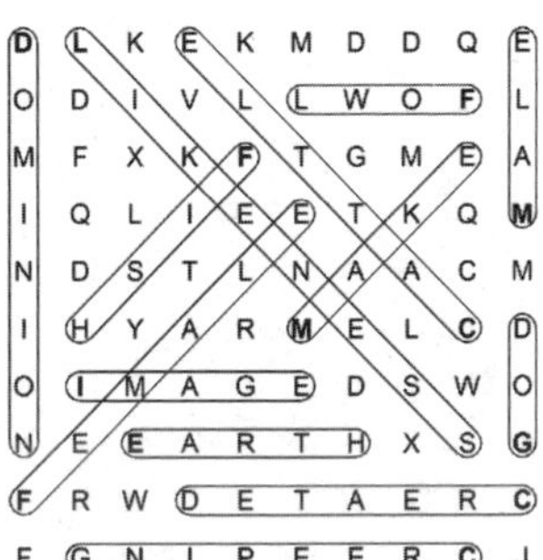

CROSSWORD

3. Creation Week

CROSSWORD

4. The Seventh Day of Creation

COLORING PAGE

5. Adam, Eve, and the Serpent

ANSWERS

WORD SEARCH

6. The First Sin

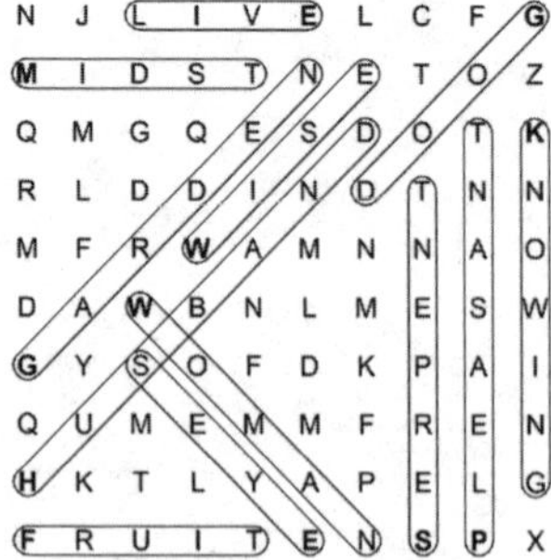

WORD SEARCH

7. Trees of the Bible

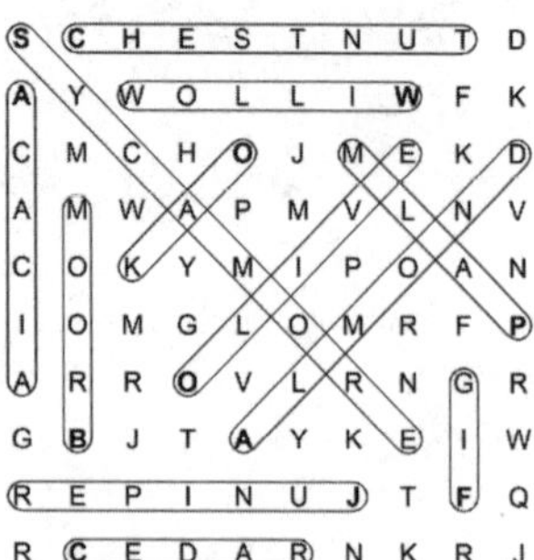

ACROSTIC

8. Building the Ark

GOPHER / ROOMS / OUTSIDE / CUBITS / THREE / FIFTY / WINDOW / SHALL

Thus Noah did,
according to all that God
commanded him, so he did.
GENESIS 6:22 SKJV

CROSSWORD

9. Boarding the Ark

COLORING PAGE

10. Noah and the Rainbow

ANSWERS

DECODER

11. God's Promise to Noah

"While the earth remains, seedtime and harvest, and cold and heat, and summer and winter, and day and night shall not cease."
GENESIS 8:22 SKJV

ACROSTIC

12. At a Place Called Babel

WHOLE / FOUND / BLOCKS / CITY / PEOPLE / MIX / UNDERSTAND / BUILDING

So the name of the city was Babel, because there the Lord mixed up the language of the whole earth.
GENESIS 11:9 NLV

CROSSWORD

13. Abram's New Name

DECODER

14. Joseph's New Coat

Now Israel loved Joseph more than all his children, because he was the son of his old age, and he made him a coat of many colors.
GENESIS 37:3 SKJV

MAZE

15. Find Baby Moses' Way to Pharaoh's Daughter

ANSWERS

WORD SEARCH

16. Baby in a Basket

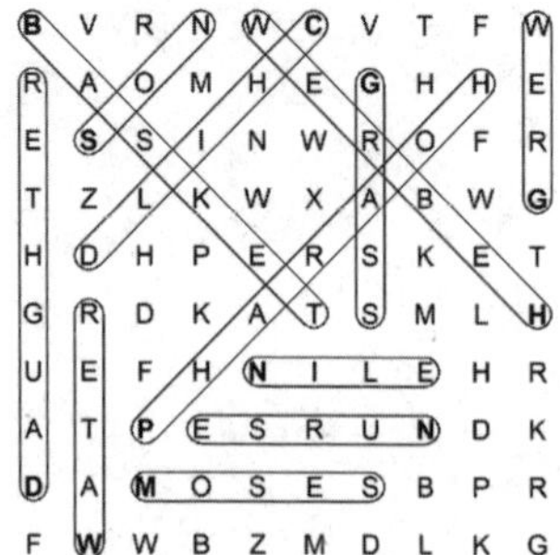

CROSSWORD

17. Plagues in Egypt

DECODER

18. Parting the Sea

And the people of Israel went through the sea on dry land. The waters were like a wall to them on their right and on their left.

Exodus 14:22 NLV

ACROSTIC

19. Miriam's Song

PHARAOH / DRY / SPOKE / DANCING / TIMBREL / AARON / FOLLOWED

"Sing to the Lord, for He is praised for His greatness."

Exodus 15:21 NLV

COLORING PAGE

20. Moses and the Ten Commandments

ANSWERS

WORD SEARCH

21. The Day of Rest

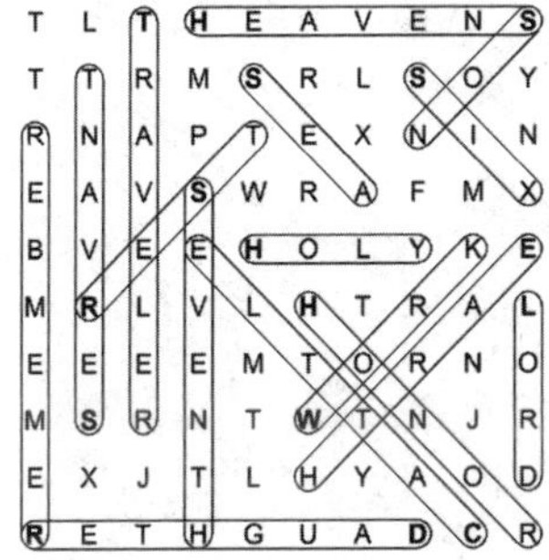

DECODER

22. The Lord in Cloud and Fire

For the cloud of the LORD was on the tabernacle by day, and fire was on it by night, in the sight of all the house of Israel, throughout all their journeys.

EXODUS 40:38 SKJV

ACROSTIC

23. Water from a Rock

BROTHER / FACES / GLORY / TAKE / ASSEMBLY / DRINK

And Moses took the rod from before the LORD, as He commanded him.

NUMBERS 20:9 SKJV

WORD SEARCH

24. The Talking Donkey

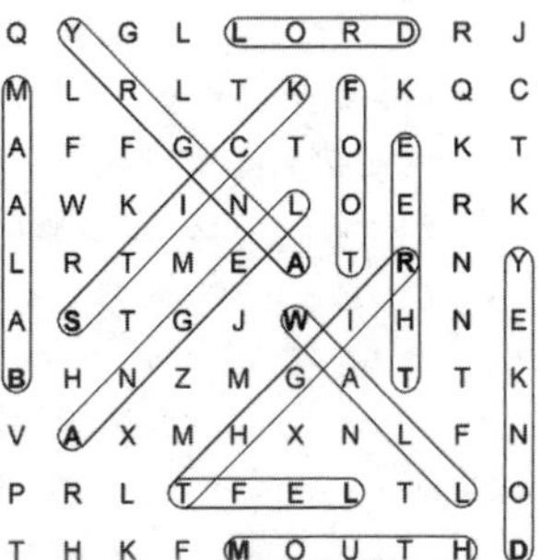

COLORING PAGE

25. Balaam, His Donkey, and the Angel

ANSWERS

ACROSTIC

26. Loving and Obeying God

LOVE / SOUL / HEART /
CHILDREN / HOUSE / GATES

"Hear, O Israel! The Lord
our God is one Lord!"
DEUTERONOMY 6:4 NLV

CROSSWORD

27. Do Not Fear

DECODER

28. A Call for Courage

"Have I not told you? Be strong
and have strength of heart!
Do not be afraid or lose faith.
For the Lord your God is with
you anywhere you go."
JOSHUA 1:9 NLV

CROSSWORD

29. Spying Out the Land

COLORING PAGE

30. Joshua and the Battle of Jericho

ANSWERS

WORD SEARCH

31. Instructions About Jericho

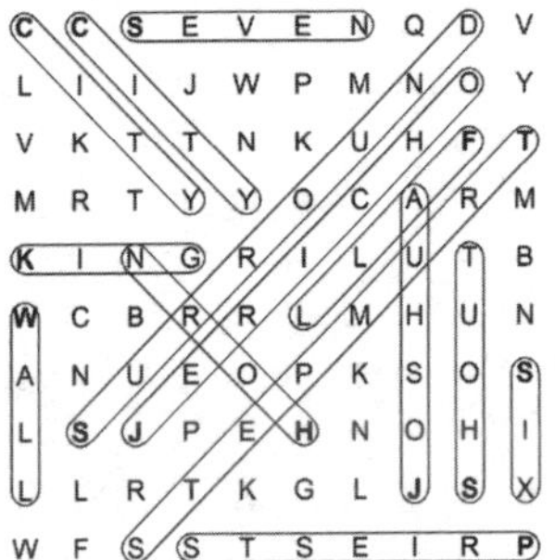

CROSSWORD

32. Jericho Falls!

WORD SEARCH

33. The Sun Stands Still

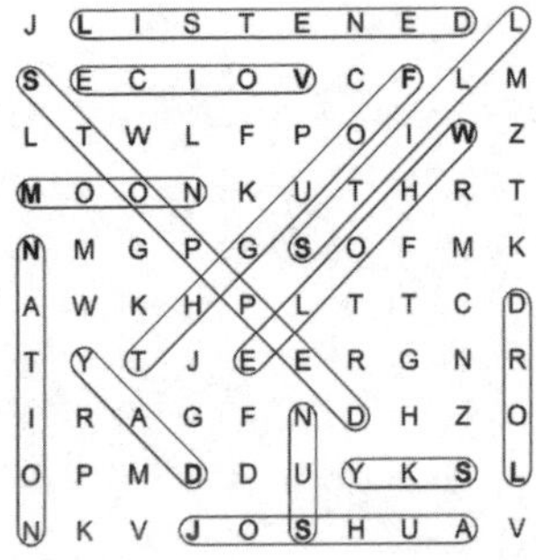

DECODER

34. Joshua Chooses the Lord

"If you think it is wrong to
serve the Lord, choose today
whom you will serve. . . .
But as for me and my family,
we will serve the Lord."

JOSHUA 24:15 NLV

COLORING PAGE

35. Samson and Delilah

ANSWERS

ACROSTIC

36. Strong Man Samson

LION / HONEY / FOXES / GRAIN / ROPES / JAWBONE / HAIR / PHILISTINES / JUDAH

And he judged Israel
in the days of the
Philistines twenty years.
JUDGES 15:20 KJV

WORD SEARCH

37. Samson's Downfall

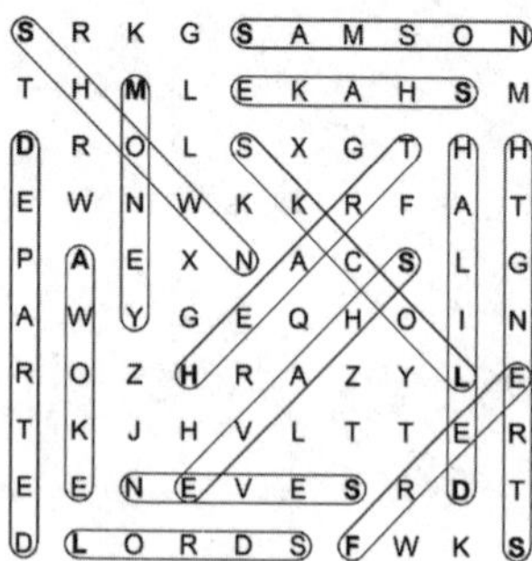

CROSSWORD

38. Ruth's Hardship

WORD SEARCH

39. Bible Grains and Plants

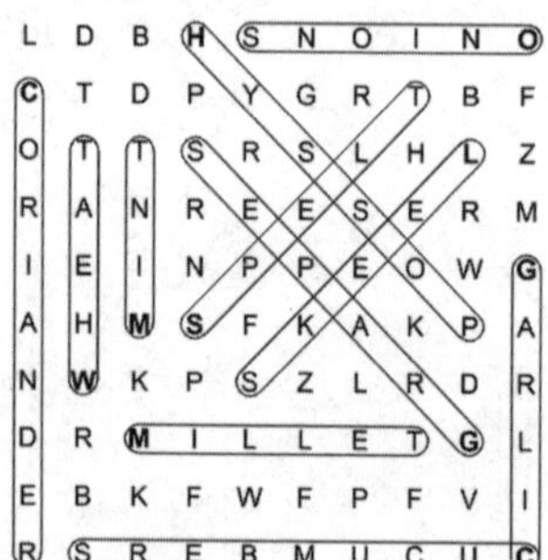

CONNECT THE DOTS

40. Ruth and Boaz

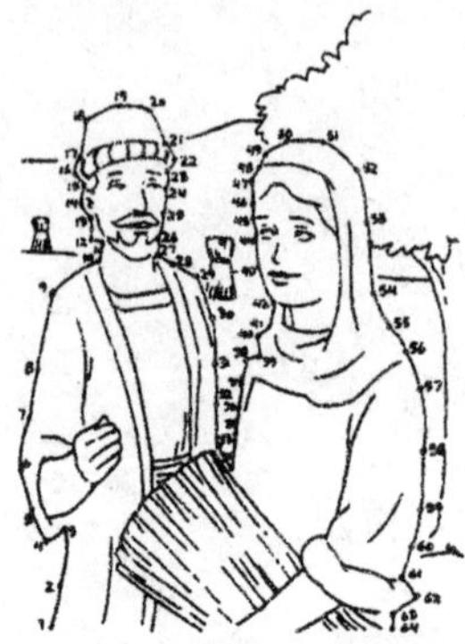

ANSWERS

WORD SEARCH

41. A Basket of Barley

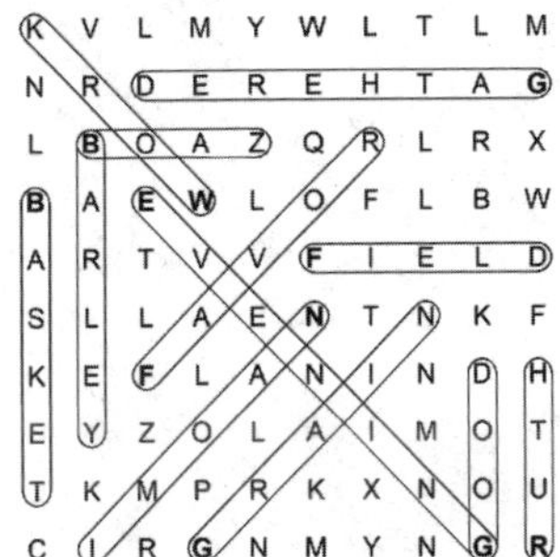

DECODER

42. Boaz and Ruth

"And now, my daughter, fear not. I will do for you all that you require, for all the city of my people know that you are a virtuous woman."
RUTH 3:11 SKJV

DECODER

43. Hannah's Thanks to God

There is no one holy like the LORD, for there is no one besides You, nor is there any rock like our God.
1 SAMUEL 2:2 SKJV

WORD SEARCH

44. God Calls to Samuel

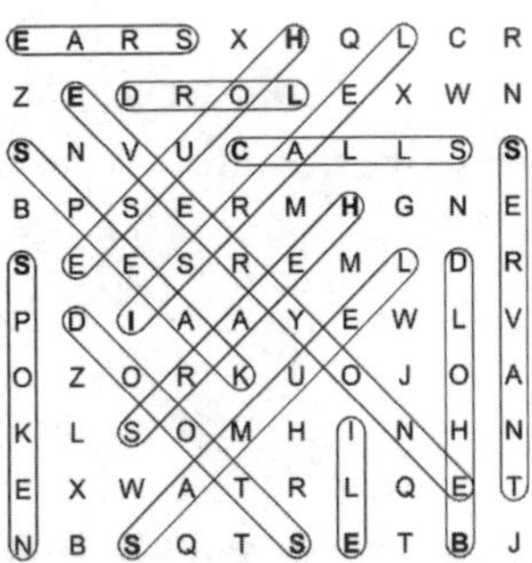

COLORING PAGE

45. Little Samuel

ANSWERS

ACROSTIC

46. Israel's First King

HEAD / YOUNG /
KISH / SERVANT / OF /
SAMUEL / WENT / HEART /
BENJAMIN / BAGS

Saul was forty years old when he began to rule. He ruled over Israel thirty-two years.

1 Samuel 13:1 NLV

CROSSWORD

47. All About David

DECODER

48. The Lord Sees the Heart

"For the Lord does not look at the things man looks at. A man looks at the outside of a person, but the Lord looks at the heart."

1 Samuel 16:7 NLV

WORD SEARCH

49. Other Good Kings of the Bible

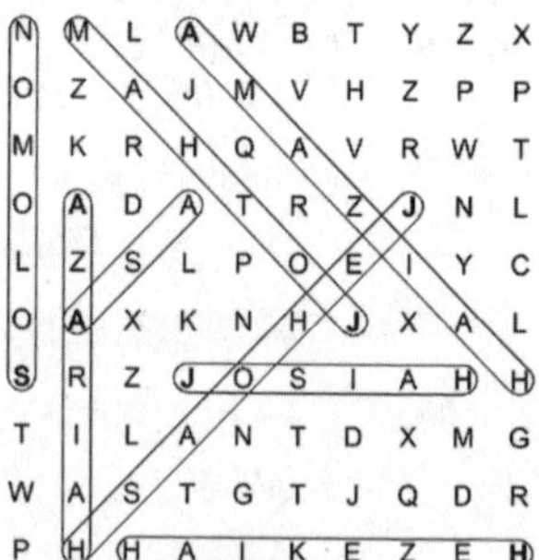

COLORING PAGE

50. David and Goliath

ANSWERS

ACROSTIC

51. A Giant Enemy

FIGHTER / NAME / PHILISTINES / TWICE / HEAD / WORE / SILVER / CARRY

Again the Philistine said, "I stand against the army of Israel this day. Give me a man, that we may fight together."
1 Samuel 17:10 NLV

DECODER

52. David's Warning for Goliath

Then David said to the Philistine, "You come to me with a sword and with a spear and with a shield. But I come to you in the name of the Lord of hosts, the God of the armies of Israel, whom you have defied."
1 Samuel 17:45 SKJV

WORD SEARCH

53. David Defeats Goliath

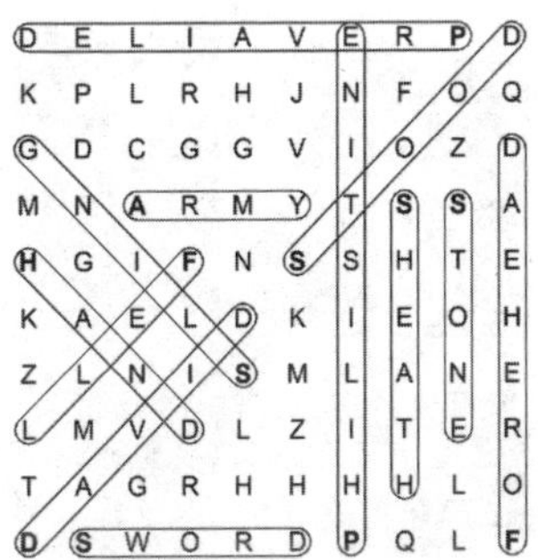

CROSSWORD

54. Celebrating David's Victory

COLORING PAGE

55. King David

ANSWERS

CROSSWORD

56. Israel's Greatest King

DECODER

57. David's Song

The LORD is my rock and my fortress and my deliverer. . . . I will call on the LORD, who is worthy to be praised, so I shall be saved from my enemies.

2 SAMUEL 22:2, 4 SKJV

WORD SEARCH

58. Solomon Asks for Wisdom

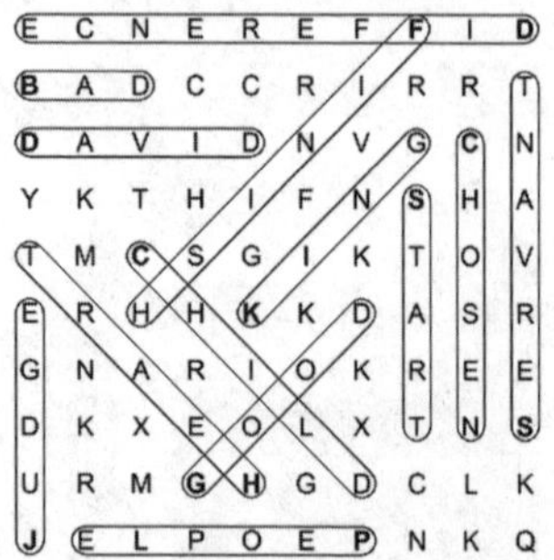

CROSSWORD

59. Building God's Temple

COLORING PAGE

60. Ravens Feed Elijah

ANSWERS

DECODER

61. Elijah and the Ravens

And the word of the Lord came to him, saying, "Leave here and turn east. Hide yourself by the river Cherith, east of the Jordan. You will drink from the river. And I have told the ravens to bring food to you there."
1 Kings 17:2–4 NLV

ACROSTIC

62. A Boy Comes Back to Life

HOUSE / BREATH / ELIJAH / GIVE / CARRIED / WOMAN / LIFE

The Lord heard the voice of Elijah. And the life of the child returned to him and he became strong again.
1 Kings 17:22 NLV

ACROSTIC

63. Elijah on Mount Carmel

EVENING / PROPHET / PRAYED / TURNED / FELL / CONSUMED / WATER

And when all the people saw it, they fell on their faces. And they said, "The Lord, He is God; the Lord, He is God."
1 Kings 18:39 SKJV

DECODER

64. Nehemiah and the King

And I said to the king, "If it pleases the king, and if your servant has found favor in your eyes, send me to Judah, to the city of my fathers' graves. Let me build it again."
Nehemiah 2:5 NLV

WHAT DOESN'T BELONG?

65. Nehemiah Rebuilds the Walls of Jerusalem

ANSWERS

CROSSWORD

66. Celebrating the Wall

CROSSWORD

67. Mordecai and Esther

DECODER

68. A Bold Request

Queen Esther answered, "If I have found favor in your eyes, O king. . .I ask that my life and the lives of my people be saved."

Esther 7:3 NLV

WORD SEARCH

69. The Jews Celebrate

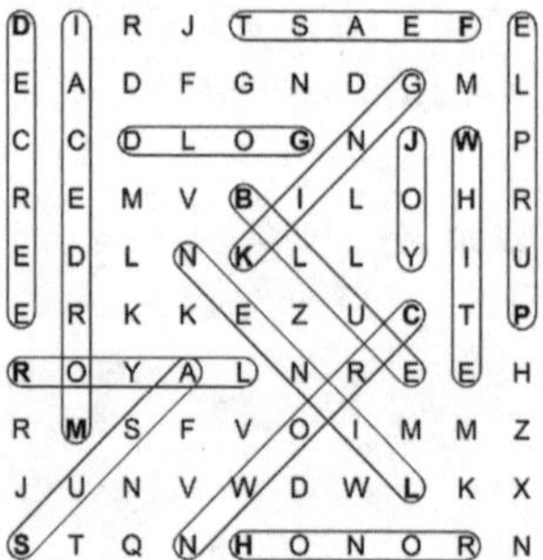

FINISH THE PICTURE

70. Queen Esther

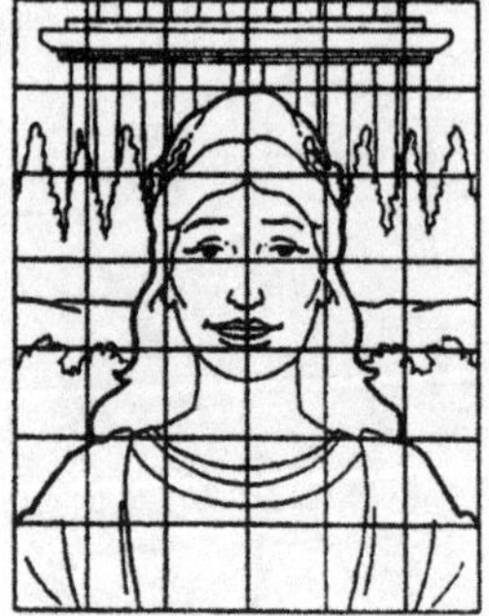

ANSWERS

WORD SEARCH

71. You Are Unique. . . and Loved

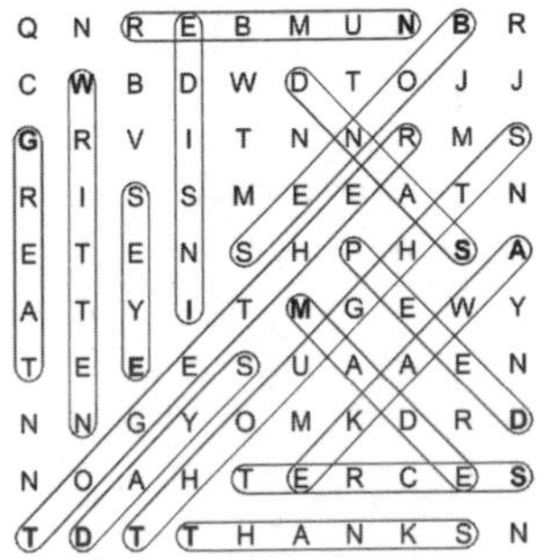

DECODER

72. Trust God's Way

Trust in the LORD with all your heart and do not lean on your own understanding. In all your ways acknowledge Him, and He shall direct your paths.
PROVERBS 3:5–6 SKJV

CROSSWORD

73. Strength for the Weary

DECODER

74. Jeremiah's Calling

Now the Word of the Lord came to me saying, "Before I started to put you together in your mother, I knew you. Before you were born, I set you apart as holy."
JEREMIAH 1:4–5 NLV

COLORING PAGE

75. Shadrach, Meshach, and Abednego

ANSWERS

ACROSTIC

76. Worship Only God

MESHACH / WORSHIP / BURNING / FLUTE / KING / DELIVER / THY

But if not, be it known unto thee, O king, that we will not serve thy gods, nor worship the golden image which thou hast set up.

DANIEL 3:18 KJV

WORD SEARCH

77. Daniel and the Lions

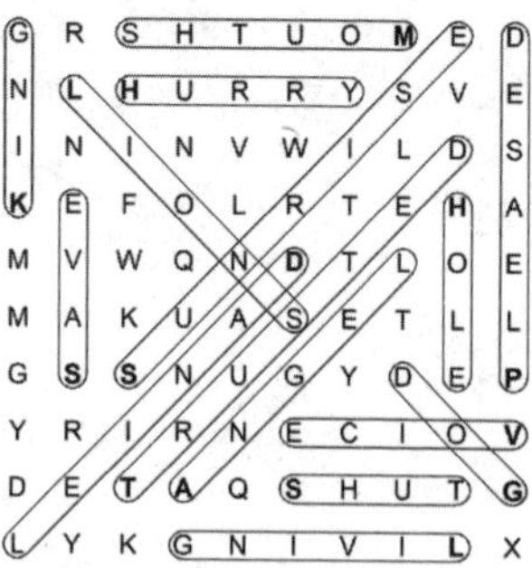

DECODER

78. God's Desire

For I desired mercy, and not sacrifice; and the knowledge of God more than burnt offerings.

HOSEA 6:6 KJV

CROSSWORD

79. Seeking Good

COLORING PAGE

80. Jonah and the Big Fish

ANSWERS

ACROSTIC

81. Jonah Disobeys God

POWERFUL / SAILORS / GOD / HEAVY / JONAH / CAPTAIN / DREW / BLAME

Jonah said to them, "I am a Hebrew, and I worship the Lord God of heaven Who made the sea and the dry land."
JONAH 1:9 NLV

DECODER

82. Fish Swallows Man!

Now the LORD had prepared a great fish to swallow Jonah. And Jonah was in the belly of the fish three days and three nights.
JONAH 1:17 SKJV

WORD SEARCH

83. Living Creatures of the Bible

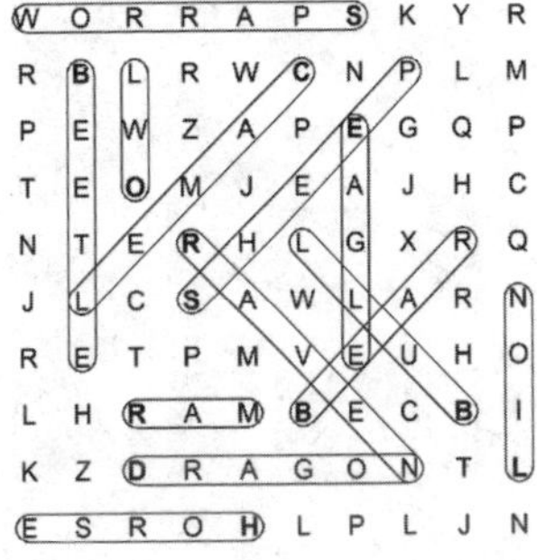

ACROSTIC

84. Prayer from a Dark Place

JONAH / PRAYED / FLOODS / TEMPLE / SOUL / THANKFUL / SALVATION

And the LORD spoke to the fish, and it vomited out Jonah on the dry land.
JONAH 2:10 SKJV

MAZE

85. Jonah Runs from God

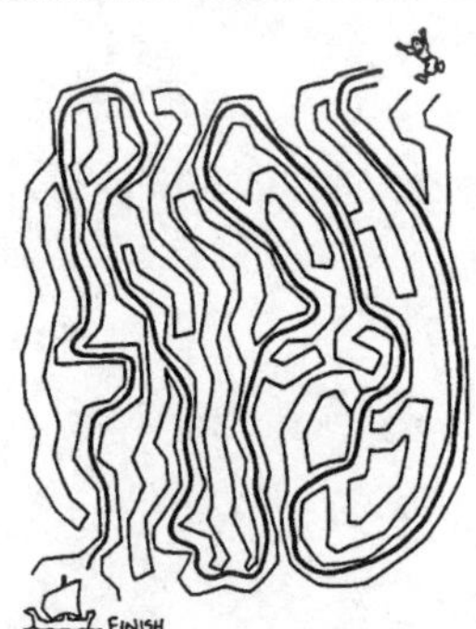

ANSWERS

DECODER

86. How to Live

He has shown you, O man, what is good. And what does the Lord require of you, but to act justly and to love mercy and to walk humbly with your God?

Micah 6:8 SKJV

DECODER

87. Our Safe Place

The Lord is good, a safe place in times of trouble. And He knows those who come to Him to be safe.

Nahum 1:7 NLV

CROSSWORD

88. Joy in the Lord

CROSSWORD

89. Jesus Is Born

COLORING PAGE

90. Christmas Visitors

ANSWERS

ACROSTIC

91. Wise Men Visit Jesus

SECRETLY / STAR /
BETHLEHEM / WORSHIP /
EAST / YOUNG / GOLD

And being warned by God in a dream that they should not return to Herod, they departed to their own country another way.
MATTHEW 2:12 SKJV

ACROSTIC

92. Be Salt and Light

EARTH / SALT / AWAY / OF /
MOUNTAIN / UNDER / GIVES

"Let your light shine in front of men. Then they will see the good things you do and will honor your Father Who is in heaven."
MATTHEW 5:16 NLV

DECODER

93. The Golden Rule

"Therefore, in all things, whatever you want men to do to you, do even so to them, for this is the Law and the Prophets."
MATTHEW 7:12 SKJV

ACROSTIC

94. Jesus Is Baptized

JOHN / WORLD / IMPORTANT /
BEFORE / ABOUT / HOLY /
GOD / BAPTIZES

"I saw this happen. I am now saying that Jesus is the Son of God."
JOHN 1:34 NLV

COLORING PAGE

95. Jesus' Baptism

ANSWERS

WORD SEARCH

96. Sweet Freedom

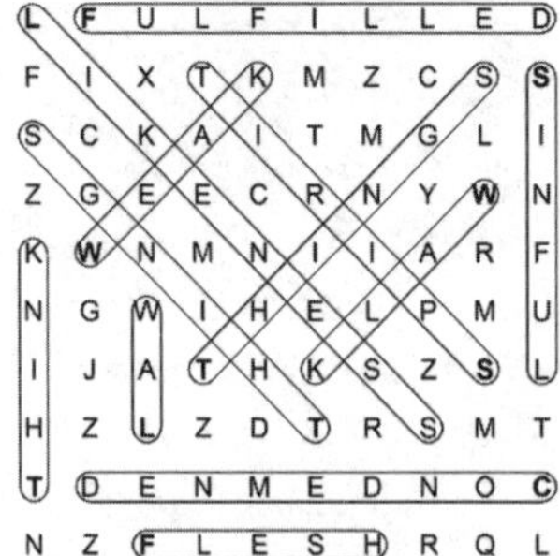

CROSSWORD

97. True Love

WORD SEARCH

98. What to Think About

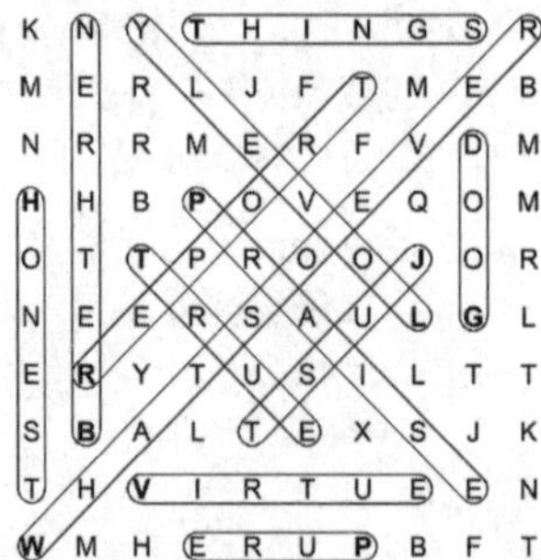

ACROSTIC

99. Saul's Change of Heart

ANANIAS / JESUS /
HOLY / FELL / BAPTIZED /
STRENGTHENED / DAMASCUS

And immediately he preached
Christ in the synagogues.
ACTS 9:20 SKJV

COLORING PAGE

100. Saul Is Saved

ANSWERS

COLORING PAGE

101. Jesus Loves You!

More Great Bible Fun!

Perfect for the 6-to-10 crowd, *On-the-Go Bible Games & Activities for Kids* promises hours of scripture-based entertainment and education. With well over 100 activities—including crosswords, word searches, secret codes, fill-in-the-blanks, and coloring pages—this book is based on passages from the very important epistle to the Romans.

Paperback / ISBN 979-8-89151-025-8